"A lot of good will come from reading this book, for both men and women, in understanding intimate relationships."

Anne McCaffrey
International best-selling author

"Almost everyone has an intuitive interest in love. Susan Edwards succeeds in achieving a task many psychologists would not attempt—to invite the reading public to enter the world of men who value love. Some of these men were born loving; others having experienced trauma, fought to regain their tender feelings; still others used love to motivate them to improve the world. Regardless of the constraints required by such stories, they are fascinating and filled with hope."

Steven F. Cohn
Professor of Sociology
University of Maine

"This is a book for the 21st century . . . a gem! The personal stories of men from all walks of life are iconic, and in many ways archetypal. Dr. Edwards infuses energy into mere words. She does not simply describe life histories; the way in which she verbally sculpts them instructs us. While always the consummate therapist, we see not therapy of trite insight, but wisdom."

Robert E. Haskell, Ph.D.
Professor of Psychology
University of New England

"A beautiful book . . . a clear style that encourages the reader to keep on reading."

C. Gilbert & Kathleen Wrenn
Originators of the Gilbert & Kathleen Wrenn
Humanitarian & Caring Person Award
American Counseling Association

" *When Men Believe in Love* is a literary 'breath of fresh air'; a beautiful, exciting and passionate collage composed of intimate glimpses into the thinking, emotions and behaviors of men who not only believe in love but also are able to translate this belief into positive interactions and relationships with women. This book breaks new ground in the age old story of the relationship between men and women and in so doing provides its readers, both male and female, with hope for a more positive future. "

Professor Douglas R. Gross, Ph.D.
Division of Psychology in Education
Arizona State University

WHEN MEN BELIEVE IN LOVE

Susan Edwards was born in York, Pennsylvania. As a child she wrote stories and poems and spent much time outdoors exploring the beauty of nature. She had a curious mind and was always asking questions about why things were the way they were and how they worked.

When she graduated with her Ph.D., she was one of forty doctorates awarded from Arizona State University, a school with 40, 000 students. Her graduate education includes two master's degrees and a Ph.D. from Arizona State University, an American-Psychological-Association approved program; the exchange doctoral student program at the University of Minnesota; two years of the Radcliffe Poetry Seminar; and a post-doctoral fellowship at Rutgers University.

Her professional background includes twenty years of contribution to the field: elementary school counseling, university teaching, industrial consultation, community psychology, inpatient and outpatient treatment, and private practice in psychology. She has received several awards in her field; published numerous articles in professional journals; written a psychology management column for the *Portland Business Journal* and is a regular consumer psychology contributor to *Custom Builder Magazine*. In addition, she has made several radio and television appearances and runs seminars for men on understanding love relationships with women.

Dr Edwards is now a licensed psychologist in Princeton, New Jersey. A multimodal psychologist with several clinical and consultative specialties, she is a member of the American Psychological Association, the American Counseling Association, and the American Association of Press Women.

When Men Believe in
LOVE

A BOOK
FOR MEN
WHO LOVE WOMEN
& THE WOMEN
THEY LOVE

Susan Edwards, Ph.D.

ELEMENT
Shaftesbury, Dorset ● Rockport, Massachusetts
Brisbane, Queensland

First published in Great Britain in 1995 by
Element Books Limited
Shaftesbury, Dorset

Published in the USA in 1995 by
Element, Inc.
42 Broadway, Rockport, MA 01966

Published in Australia in 1995 by
Element Books Limited
for Jacaranda Wiley Limited
33 Park Road, Milton, Brisbane 4064

2/96

$19.95

Cover design by Max Fairbrother
Design by Roger Lightfoot
Typeset by ROM-Data Corporation, Falmouth, Cornwall
Printed and bound in Great Britain by
Redwood Books Ltd, Trowbridge, Wiltshire

British Library Cataloguing in Publication
data available

Library of Congress Cataloging in Publication
data available

ISBN 1–85230–619–X

Bookstore

Contents

To men
   whose kindness I respect
   whose vulnerability I value
   and whose ability to grow places me in awe.

In Memoriam   and in the world

   Charles, my grandfather   Merrill and Art, my uncles
   Bill, my grandpa   Dave and Scott, my cousins
   Walter, Lee, Ed, my uncles   Tommy Stetler, my first
   Fred, my Dad   boyfriend
                                Scott Wallace, my high school
                                   sweetheart
                                my friends Steve, Billy, Jay,
                                   Greg, Peter, Brad and their
                                   sons
                                my friends Dwight, Jack, Brian,
                                   Dan, Hans and Justin
                                Doug, Gilbert & Arnold, my
                                   teachers

and to my colleagues, former students, patients and other
men of honor who have the courage to still believe in love.

                              from Susan, 1995

Men Who Believe in Love

Devastated, he was,
when his son died
and his tears splashed
over the next ten years. He
was Sam.

Sad, he was,
when he couldn't read
and his teachers punished him
as his aloneness moved him through time
until he was a man.
He was Daniel.

Frightened, he was,
when at seventeen
he ran between grenades in Indochina
and shivered in the fire
of the night.
He was Greg.

Honored, he was,
when he graduated,
doctorate in hand.
He went to the university
and they slew him.
He was Jack.

Loved nature, he did,
and as a kid played in the woods
and ran wild up the hill
and they dressed him in a suit
and told him
to behave.
He was Jay.

And Walter,
who lost his folks,
both of them,
within two weeks.
And he cried.

The stories go on
and the courage
welled up from inside
and they learned the pain
of being a man
and the power
of stitching lifewill
with belief
in love.

Foreword

Author's Note: This is a book about men who love. Men who are real. It is not about men who pretend or who hide. It is not about men who say one thing but do another. It is about men—whether evolving into their loving selves or having already developed them fully—who love. It is written by a psychologist, but is not about theory. It is about life.

For all those reasons, I asked that the foreword be written by a man who is real, a man who loves. I wanted the book from page one to be a mirror for that which is.

The foreword is presented by Mr. Harry Jansen. He is a retired police officer with 33 years' service in the state of Wisconsin, but he is perhaps best known as the father of the United States Olympic speed skater, gold medalist Dan Jansen, whose victory in the 1994 Olympics in Lillehammer, Norway, touched the hearts of the American people. Most of the American viewing public can recall Dan Jansen's victory lap around the ice, holding his infant daughter Jane in his arms, in honor of his sister of the same name who died of leukemia in 1988. Mr. Jansen was there through it all. His comments about the book and about love follow.

I've recognized from my experience on the police force that men sometimes leave their families. After reading this book I now understand why.

The situation I ran into was this. The relationship would be going good, and all of a sudden the man would become real mean and not show up anymore. The woman often was at a loss to interpret it. She didn't know why; she had no idea. She didn't know what she had done. I really didn't know the reason either. When we got there, the woman stated that things were going well and all of a sudden, he just turned sour. I found the woman tended to blame herself and figured it must have been her fault. I realize now after reading this book that the man was afraid of love. He was falling in love and was afraid. He didn't know how to handle it.

I enjoyed reading the book and had to remind myself it was written by a psychologist because it read so smoothly. It kept my interest and I found myself looking forward to turning the page to see what happened next. This is a collection of men's lives captured in stories and the way Susan Edwards has interwoven the case histories makes it easier to understand. Some of the difficulties these men overcame were overwhelming.

I've seen men turn their lives around like Howard Schukowski did in Chapter 9. Many times in my career I've seen men in trouble like that—heavy drinkers or those who had problems with the law—who get married and you think it won't last. But they had love as motivation—they change— and we (the police) never see them again. They turn out to be good family men. That's what it's all about—love as motivation. What I've seen in real life many times is reflected here within the pages of a book.

The description of imagery as a process within the mind interested me, too. We lost a daughter, and when I go to a wedding, I remember how she looked when she got married. When I attend a graduation, I can picture her when she graduated from nurses' training. These mental pictures stay with you. What you try to do is reweave them into understanding.

I was in Austria on February 14, 1989, with the United States World Cup Skating Team. Dan was competing, and it was the one-year anniversary of Jane's death. I stayed by myself and just walked in the streets. When something like that happens, you think, "Why me?" But you realize you have to go on. I think seeing how other people have solved their problems gives people hope. And some of the problems are quite serious.

To me part of courage is keeping your loving self. I've felt this way. My son Dan's courage to go on inspires respect. In the 1988 Olympics he skated the day his sister died. He fell. And he fell a week later, too. It's a wonder he could go out on

the ice at all. But he did it for himself and his family and his sister. I could see that in him. I call it courage and I told him that at that time. I think it is important for men to see their own courage. Emotional courage is required for life. It is part of being a man.

Harry Jansen

Preface

I have always had an interest in men and love.

As a child I had a sensitive nature—my Dad said I was just born that way. As a little girl I valued beauty. The romantic classics of childhood and the loving men in my life were part of the beauty that painted my early world.

As a teenager I was awestruck by the writers and poets of world literature, many of whom were men. And I remember how much my worldview changed when I realized in kindergarten that classmate Tommy Stetler was my boyfriend and later, after the senior prom, when Scott Wallace and I kissed. For whatever reason, over the years my interest in men and love has remained.

I suppose men will say things to a doctor they will not share with anyone else. And when they have spoken, I have listened. For the last twenty years, in fact, men have talked with me about love.

To some I was a doctor. To others I was a teacher at the local university. Still others read my newspaper column. Some attended my seminars and speeches; others were individuals I interviewed. Some men whose stories have touched me deeply are close friends; others were strangers who simply spoke with me as the passenger seated next to them in an airplane. To some I was a poet; to others the girl next door who was now grown up. What I am is a psychologist.

Psychologists attempt to explain people: how they act, what they feel and why they do the things they do. Psychologists are trained to view people from the inside out. That is what makes the field unique. It looks at thoughts, feelings, actions, motivations and other elements of personality and integrates these into a meaningful whole. Within the historical context of medicine this field remains relatively new, so the ideas that explain human behavior are still evolving. There is much we have to learn.

This book is about men who value love with women. It is based on some of the things I have learned over the course of my career and addresses some of the conditions within men who believe in love. It shares their stories and allows us to see inside their worlds. Included are personal struggle and victory; shame and sadness; joy and pleasure. Some of the words are their own.

All of the stories in this book are true. For the sake of privacy, names and identifying factors have been changed to accommodate the wishes of the individuals involved. The remaining stories are used with their permission. This is a book whose mirror reflects courage and whose message is about hope—hope for love.

What I have attempted to do is to summarize what I have learned from and about the situation that exists when men believe in love. It is different from what happens when they don't.

Acknowledgments

To the members of the goodness network who support my life. Your help has made this book possible.

To Mom, who was my best teacher. Your love and encouragement has made a difference in my life.

To the members of my family, in memoriam, my extended family and especially three aunts who always believed in me—Margaret, Ruth and Mildred.

To the members of my honorary family

Sisters:
Susan Cornman, J.D., encourager; Jean Ashland, Ph.D., honorary good fairy; Debbie Skibbee, Ph.D., empathy plus; Barbara Harrison, Ph.D., kindness; Pat B., Ph.D., true friend; Susan O., the other one; Liz Silverman, honorary little sister; Claudia Hanstveit and her daughter Sophie, who make me laugh; Carol Stein Gottschalk and Cathy Zehnder Perich, friends from high school who are kin in my heart; Nancy Neutz, pure goodness; Margaret Murray of the twinkling eyes; Sally Hayman, my spunky sister; Elvia my cheerleader; Anne Carroll Fowler, Ph.D., friend and poet; Heather Thompson, Tina Luce, and Patrice Hampson, valued friends; and Shauna Salerno, stepmother to my thirty-year-old horse Done Pleased.

Brothers of the heart:
those to whom the book is dedicated, whose poems appear

on these pages and those whose kindness touches my life in a rainbow of light.

To Emmy, Velma, Steven, Joe, Rose, Ella, Brian, Jack and others whose identity need not be shared within these pages but to whom much appreciation has been expressed.

And to Susan McCoy, MD, and her office staff Patti, JoAnne and Allie; Pam Smith; and Lynne Cohne in the Carrier Library—all aglow with expertise and support plus.

And to my editor Julia and publisher Michael who really do believe in love.

Thank you from my heart.

PART ONE

To Love or Not to Love?

1 When Men Believe in Love

"That I can love," he said, "is the greatest victory of my life." David paused and added thoughtfully,

> That I believe in love is something beyond victory.
>
> I wanted to die when I was five. My mother leaned me against the back of our house and whipped my buttocks with a stick until I urinated against the wall. She screamed shaming insults at me while quoting the Bible, and she mocked me. I was her prisoner for years. My father wasn't home much, but my grandparents loved me. I was a lonely little boy.

Psychological aloneness haunted David like a restless wind in the attic. He was grown up by the time we met, and we have been friends for twenty years. That he is kind is a victory. That he is loving is amazing. I still don't understand exactly how he did it, but as a psychologist I have some ideas. There is something about human victory basic to empowerment, and something about personal empowerment fundamental to psychology and to the ability to love.

THE SCIENCE OF VICTORY

In order to explain David's psychological victory, we need to develop a paradigm—a model that provides a sort of idea window through which to look. Paradigms weave together ideas, theory and research on human behavior to help us grow in understanding.

Paradigms have always existed in the history of science. And, like the clothes we wore in high school, we often outgrow them. Years ago before antibiotics were understood, physicians in the American Civil War treated open wounds on soldiers with a certain kind of moss. These soldiers recovered better than those who had no moss. The model (or paradigm) was that moss helped the wounds heal more fully. Years later it was discovered that it was not the moss but an agent in the moss that helped heal the wounds. That agent is known today as an antibiotic. Consequently, the paradigm changed. Healing that was credited to moss was replaced with a new explanation: antibiotics.

One of the most widely read writers in the history of science, Thomas Kuhn, author of *The Structure of Scientific Revolutions* (1962: University of Chicago Press, Chicago), writes that science advances by continuing to outgrow its paradigms. What we think is true at one time allows us to discover something else that is true at a later time. As a result, we often reject what we once accepted as true. This is how we grow in knowledge and understanding.

Understanding people is very difficult because there are so many things that affect them. So our models are often imperfect in predicting how people will act or in explaining why they do the things they do. As we continue to learn, we develop models we will someday outgrow. And we are helped by the life stories of people like David.

From a field called risk research, the study of resilience offers one such paradigm. In Chapter 4 I have utilized it to explain how David achieved the ability to love when his history was so abusive. It is one of the paradigms in psychology that explains empowerment and psychological victory over profound adversity. I have applied it to men who love. Their victory can be understood and similarly achieved by others.

LOVE AND NATURE

From the time Shane first peered out into the big world, he had a sparkle in his eye. And it became brighter. Some men are just born loving. His father said,

> Shane was born with a loving temperament, and it hasn't changed. From the time he was an infant, he watched your every move and snuggled in when you held him. He smiled after he was two months old and adapted well to new situations. Now he's nearly two and he smiles a lot. His face lights up when he sees you and he claps when something happens he likes. He laughs a lot, giggles, and says "Mama" and "Dada." He is fascinated by animals of all kinds. He gets excited and wants to touch them or play with them, but he isn't hurtful. He has a kind of happy respect for animals— he knows they're alive—and he loves imitating the sounds they make. Mostly, I guess, he's a kid who just shows joy.

People are born with different temperaments and different natural abilities. Some people are naturally athletic, a talent that is evident from the time they are young. Others may be naturally musical, artistic or mathematical. Often when someone has a strong natural ability, it is accompanied by a belief in how important it is.

Over the years, I have observed that some people have a natural ability to love. As they travel through life, their belief in love continues. Some of these people are men—men like Shane—born loving, who include in their identities, at the inner core, being loving. While they may live in all cultures, be represented by all socioeconomic levels, and interact with the world in a variety of occupations, the important thing is that they exist.

From a research perspective, such men would be classified as "true positives." That is, the way they appear to be on the outside (loving) is the way they are on the inside (loving). They choose to live their lives that way. While they are not perfect, there is something qualitatively different about them in terms of human relationships. The difference shows up most in the influence they have on others. In the garden of human relationships, such individuals are the water and the rain. The effect they have on others is nurturing.

For years social scientists have attempted to explain why people are the way they are. A controversy emerged over nature versus nurture in determining human personality and behavior, which resulted in three different theoretical positions. The first one focuses on nature and suggests that people are born with a temperament based on the influence of genetics. The second one emphasizes environment: people develop as a result of what they learn from their relationships with their parents, family, culture, and so on. The third position involves a combination of both nature and nurture.

Explaining human behavior is very difficult, partly because research on humans is so complex. In social science, unlike physical science, we are limited in how we can explain the wide variation in human behavior.

In physical science, add two atoms of hydrogen and one atom of oxygen and—given a certain temperature range—a molecule of water is created every time. Not so in trying to understand or predict human behavior. It is the scientific equivalent of ending up with water, zinc and a daffodil one time, and black sludge the next. The results are unpredictable.

How does all of this relate to men and love? This chapter presents several windows through which to view men who believe in love. Loving men seem to be created by nature, by nurture, and by a combination of both. Some were born loving and never changed. Some unearthed their own loving nature and belief in love in response to an event in their lives; and some are still in the process of discovery.

LOVE AND IDENTITY

Some men define themselves as loving. It is part of how they see themselves, and a belief in love is as basic as their understanding of the importance of breathing. They are men who, upon entering the room, bring in the sun.

My Uncle Walter was like that. He had twinkling eyes, joked and laughed with people, and was insightful about human nature. Although he'd attended college, he worked in a steel plant most of his life in a town called Steelton, Pennsylvania. He was a carpenter in his spare time and liked to fix houses.

He died after I graduated from college but what I remember most about him was the way things seemed lighter when he was around. If it was cloudy outside, his presence seemed to brighten the room. He talked with everyone, genuinely seemed to enjoy other people, smiled a lot, and had a little kid kind of laugh that started in his belly and echoed its way into his lungs. He was kind, mirthful yet serious, and loving.

He loved my aunt and told me once he still pictured her the way he did when they dated in high school—as the leading lady in the school play.

When we were kids, he always made us laugh, but it was never at our expense. Instead of ridiculing people, he just created fun. From the moment you walked in the room, he had a way of making you feel special. He made a difference in my life, Uncle Walter did, just by being in it.

Making a difference is part of what belief in love is about for men. Jens Mortensen feels the same way. A native of Denmark, he lives in a suburb of Copenhagen today. He is a veterinarian and his father was a veterinary surgeon. Jens grew up in a family that was loving and that encouraged children to be individuals who help others. He shared his story as follows.

Every family has crises. They pop up from time to time. Even though you have serious family disagreements—even though you've been shouting from one end of the house to another—the next day it might not be forgotten, but you know that underneath there is still love. Sometimes you can solve problems. Sometimes they can't be solved, but you figure out ways to live with the difficulties, even though you might think the person is wrong in some ways. You don't let problems undermine your sense of the good in relationships.

I think men have the right to be strong and they also have the right to be weak and soft—it's not a source of shame. It's not considered bad if a boy cries. Men tend to have an attitude to show that they always have everything under control, but this is obviously not always the case. And it is not such a big shame nowadays if you happen to show your feelings or weak spots.

This view is shared by a lot of men here. Men share a lot in childcare, too, because most women work in Denmark. When both parents are involved with small children, it allows them to be more sentimental.

In my family it was more of an egalitarian culture. Women were viewed as equal to men. School was easy for me, and I am a mainstream Dane. My wife Alicja is a veterinarian also. She is from Poland and we met in a student exchange program. For my part, it was love at first sight. I'm not sure it was for her. We are both fond of each other and, while we won't know the end for many years, until now we are very happy.

My philosophy of life? Oh, I don't know. I have always felt it was important for a person to make a positive mark on his surroundings—whether by doing something that is useful or by being helpful or comforting to other people around you. I think I had this idea from the time I was a small child.

You will notice that Jens' views include an acceptance of strength and as well as vulnerability. Both are integrated into his identity. So is what he views as the purpose for his life.

I think it is important to make a positive mark on your surroundings. What is important to me in life is that I feel that whatever I do is useful to the company I work in and the society I am living in. In whatever a person can contribute—a story, a painting, a songwriter who writes a song—in small matters and in large matters—what you do matters somehow and does make a difference.

It is possible, then, to combine love, work and identity. Such men do. And they exist in every field, although you might be surprised at the wide range of individuals involved.

Dr. Jack Mendleson, a friend of mine who is a management professor, shared with me a quotation from a speech given by Vince Lombardi, the famous coach of the Green Bay Packers football team. The quotation, given in an address to the American Management Association, included a similar idea.

Mental toughness is humility, simplicity, Spartanism.
And, one other, love.
I don't necessarily have to like my associates, but as a
person I must love them.
Love is loyalty. Love is teamwork. Love respects the dignity
of the individual.
Heartpower is the strength of your corporation.[1]

Vince Lombardi was a legend in American sports. He was an inspirational leader, a larger-than-life presence, someone who brought love to the world of sports and business—and he made a difference.

LOVE AND PAIN

It is sometimes difficult for men to believe in love. To do so requires great courage because the experience of love can bring much pain. Devastating pain. To maintain a belief in love, a man needs to learn to deal with the potential pain of being emotionally vulnerable without surrounding his heart with armor.

I can still picture the deep, sad eyes of one young man I treated several years ago. His name was Harry, he was twelve years old, and he was referred for suicide.

Harry was referred to me for evaluation while I was a psychologist working in a clinic. He had left a crumpled suicide note in his brother's bedroom after being betrayed by his first love. He was seriously depressed and wanted to die.

Why did he want to die? He had fallen in love, and the girl had responded to him, showing affection, kissing him, giving him gifts, and making him feel cared for. Her goal, however, was not related to him. It seems she was trying to obtain his best friend. Being the girl of one young man gave her closer proximity to the other. When she achieved her goal, my patient was devastated. Harry never suspected she was anything but sincere. She had been a great actress. He was vulnerable because he really loved her.

There were tears in his eyes when he told me, "I will never again have a girlfriend."

The sadness in his young eyes is with me still, a commentary on the potential pain that accompanies the emotional vulnerability of loving. His feelings of loss, betrayal and sadness were so intense that when he looked into his future, he could not even picture a girl in it. And it was partially that empty picture of the future in his own mind that led to his wanting to die. Life is fairly bleak to a sensitive adolescent who gets a glimpse of his life as a grownup and sees that love is missing.

"I can't understand why she did that to me," he would say. "I just don't get it."

Harry entered therapy and his progress was good. It was not easy, but in the course of time he learned that not all girls were like the one who had betrayed him; some were like his cousin Rachel, honest, kind, and sincere. At the end of his treatment, he was able to see that his future could have a girl in it if she and he were alike on the inside—if they both had kind hearts.

One day he thanked me and said,

I realize that I am a kind person. I would never pretend to like someone just to get someone else. It's not right. And there are girls out there who in that way are like me. Maybe someday one of those will be my girlfriend. And in the meantime, I think it's good for me just to have good friends—and some of those are girls in my class.

Harry learned one of the most important ways of handling pain. He learned that what one person of a certain group (in

this case, a girl) does to hurt someone else in a particular group
(in this case, a boy) should not be used to categorize all
members of that particular group. All girls do not have to
be bad or hurtful. When he learned this, he became free to
hope.

*This kind of learning can also be achieved by men who were
victims of child abuse.* A man whose mother was hurtful to
him—beat him, enjoyed inflicting physical pain on him, and
hit his head against a concrete floor again and again on one
occasion—told me how he learned to love women.

Philip, now twenty-two, and living in California, is a gifted
musician and rising star in the music world. He has superior
intelligence and his music is spirited. His story is being told
using a pseudonym. After his parents die, he said, he would
like to publish it in his own name.

I was emotionally and physically traumatized most of my
childhood. There were moments of joy but the overriding
mood was one of sadness. I was beaten a lot—with a belt,
a two-foot long oak paddle, and other things as well.
Mother justified it, saying, "To spare the rod is to spoil the
child." But I don't think she worried about me becoming
spoiled. I think it had to do with maintaining a sense of
power and gaining control. You don't have to deal with
children's feelings if you treat them like a whipped dog.
Then they become very well behaved on the outside, proper,
but on the inside they are living in pain.

The amazing thing to me was that she showed no remorse
afterward. Either she felt no remorse or she had no understanding of how children feel. I also wondered whether she
got some sort of sexual high out of it—like a kind of sexual
gratification associated with the inflicting of pain on someone else. Anyhow, no matter what happened—whether I got
a sick stomach or failed a math test in school, the answer
she had was the same: problems were handled with beatings,
which were supposed to resolve everything.

"How did you ever overcome that pain?" I asked Philip one

day. He is a friend of a colleague of mine, and we were talking about men and love as we had talked on several occasions. People who didn't know him could probably scarcely imagine this dark-haired, attractive man as having suffered such personal trauma. His words were from the innermost space of the heart.

My mother was very cruel. I remember being in kindergarten when our cat was taken away. She had several of our pets put down. She would say they were "bad" and would send them to the veterinarian's to be put to sleep. She seemed to enjoy taking animals away from us. But the biggest problem I had as a child was not the victimizing of animals; it was the victimizing of me.

I felt she punished me sometimes just for fun. It was awful. I was sad, angry, and ashamed. It was so humiliating.

There were two things, I think, that helped me overcome this awful time. First, because I am an artist, I was able to retreat to the world of imagination. From an early age on, I nourished my imagination. It is very hard to put this into words, but the love I had inside of me was beautiful and just so full of life, that I knew it wasn't bad. And if it wasn't bad, neither was I. I have talked with other musicians and some of them used a similar process—tapping into the music swirling around inside them, full of such love and beauty.

I guess the other thing that broke the spell for me was seeing that there were other women in my life who liked me, treated me kindly and really seemed to care. My Aunt Mary was that way and so was my friend Mark's mother, my neighbor down the street. They both hugged me, seemed happy to see me when I showed up and smiled a lot when they talked to me. By the time I was in third grade, I knew not all women were cruel like my mother. Some of them were kind. And when I figured that out, I decided that the problem was not me. My mother's treatment continued to affect me for a long time but it did not make me hate all women or reject my own sensitive nature. And this makes me very proud.

I had tried to capture this type of psychological victory some years ago in a poem I wrote. It is dedicated to the respect that individuals like Harry, Philip and others inspire in me as a psychologist.

> *wonder child*
> *been through a*
> *cradlefire*
> *to*
> *again*
> *learn*
> *to dance.*[2]

Here we have two stories from two different young men of very different backgrounds. Both saved themselves from hating all women forever for the pain that one had caused. They learned to approach the problem differently and not to generalize. They learned that some females are cruel but more importantly, some are kind. The pain had been caused by one who was cruel. The lantern of hope was carried by those who were kind.

LOVE AND CONFUSION

Love is the chaos theory of human relationships. Daily life seems fairly lawful, organized around certain routines or principles, and then along comes love and changes everything. Sometimes a man is not aware that it is love he has run into in the course of daily life. Sometimes it is just the unknown, accompanied by a general state of confusion.

Rodney experienced such a state of confusion. He was a forty-five year old electrician who was referred by his family doctor to my office several years ago for depression. He couldn't sleep or eat and was having nightmares. A relationship with a woman he really cared about had ended. He said it ended for a matter of principle, but it was really for a matter of jealousy. When Janet, no longer in his life, started seeing someone else, his psychological defenses broke down, and his physical health declined.

"I just don't understand it," he said. "Why am I so upset? I have never been like this before, and I have ended relations with women before. There is something very different about this."

Rodney, married and divorced when he was in his early twenties, had experienced nearly twenty-five years of superficial relationships with women. His pattern was to become involved with someone, date her exclusively for a period of time, and then see someone else. He did not want a committed relationship and so did not choose it. He was, as an adult, experiencing the carefree adolescence he had never had. He had expected that pattern to continue, except that Janet interrupted the cycle.

He had not expected himself to become so attached to her. She had a small daughter, and the three of them had done things as a family. Rodney found himself responding in ways he was not used to. He found himself talking to Janet about himself and his feelings, revealing himself in ways he had never done with other women. He was used to playing the good-time Charlie role, and now he was face-to-face with a woman who was bluntly honest and expected the same thing from him. There was nowhere he could put his insecurity, and although he told her not to expect anything from him, he found himself becoming more and more involved with her.

His inner confusion—the whirling of internal feelings paired with behavior that was unusual for him—placed him in a state of panic. When the father of Janet's little girl showed up on the scene—even though it was only to maintain a parental role with the daughter and not to rekindle a romantic relationship with the mother—Rodney became very jealous. He started making accusations, discounted her affection for him, and became increasingly suspicious. When he showed up at her house, drunk, accusatory and making a scene, she had had it. She threw him out.

The confusion that plagued Rodney was this: he did not understand the depth of the caring and love he had for Janet.

He tried to keep the relationship at a surface level—dates, sex, and a "don't expect much from me" attitude—but it didn't work. He misjudged his own level of caring. When another man appeared on the scene, his insecurity about being so involved in the first place was more than he could handle. He acted out and was rejected.

Rodney didn't recognize that what he felt for Janet was love. He was so used to guarding against it that it took him by surprise. Confusion was a cloud that hung around his head; it hid the emotional attachment that existed underneath.

Rodney persisted in treatment for nearly two years. He wanted to understand what had happened to him, and what he learned in the process was fascinating. While he and Janet did not reconcile as she eventually married the man she was seeing, out of the confusion came a clarity that altered the way he lived his life. He recognized that he was trying to hide from his feelings and pretend that he was not involved when in fact he was. He learned to grieve the loss of his first love, which had been a symbolic issue in the choice to become superficially involved with women. And he was able to say goodbye to adolescence in a way that still allowed him to retain the youthful spunk that he admired within himself. Out of the confusion, he was able to forge a new sense of himself as a person, one based on respect and not using women, while running away from his own loving heart.

Rodney had always believed in love, which was why he had never fully accepted the loss of his first true love. When he was able to understand himself better, he was able to change the sequence of his own behavior patterns.

It has been nearly five years since I treated Rodney, although I hear from him now and then. He is involved in a committed relationship with a woman he loves and who appears to love him. He often looks back on the events of his life leading to therapy with surprise.

"I had no idea," he constantly says, "that so much in my life would change. It was a turning point, all right. My life was a mess, and now it's really good."

THE COURAGE TO CHOOSE LOVE

To love someone is a choice. The choice itself is not simple. Love reflects a unique personal choice. Just as all people do not like the same flavors of ice cream or agree on the best type of pet, so all individuals do not make the same choices in love.

In Norway last year, I interviewed a very interesting man who was a long-time friend of my Norwegian hosts. His story illustrates the courage to stand up for individual convictions. Fahmy shared it with me as follows.

> Translated, my name means "The Sword of Mohammed." I am Muslim—a moderate Muslim—and I was born in Egypt. I left there at twenty-two to pursue my career dream of photography. My quest took me to England where I studied cinema and then to Norway as I ended up marrying a Norwegian woman. I am thirty-nine and never would have expected that my life would have taken the turns that it has.
>
> When I met Reidun (my wife), I knew right away that I liked her. She was so honest and I immediately felt comfortable with her. We were from cultures that were just about as different as they could be, but we both have come to understand much better the world in which each of us was raised. There have been adjustments on each of our parts and cross-cultural issues which posed obstacles. But we have managed to adapt in the twelve years we have been with each other because we want to be together.

How did Fahmy show courage? In spite of all of the difficulties facing him—cultural, geographical, emotional, economic and even historical—he chose love.

He explained it this way:

> One of the biggest adjustments I had to make was related to culture. In Arab lands, jealousy played a big part; men were very possessive of women. Then here I was, meeting a Scandinavian who believed in freedom. It was tough. And

she is very pretty. So, I had to adjust. She handled it in a good way—I knew she cared about me and she tried to please me—and we learned to compromise on things.

I also had to learn how to share my feelings. In Egypt, feelings are kept on the inside, people don't show them in public. If something happens, one didn't dare to talk about it. With Reidun I had to learn that it made us closer when I talked about how I felt about something.

I am still close with my family in Egypt, and Reidun is close with her family here. And they have learned to accept each other's spouse because that person makes us happy. In that way, we are lucky. Both families love us and our children—Sandra and Ramy. And they want our children to be happy. As a man, I am a romantic. As a father, I take my role seriously. My life here is certainly well worth the adjustments I have made along the way. Somehow, it just works out.

LOVE AND RISK

Many times love doesn't work because one has an expectation of "safe-love." That is, one expects that love can be obtained without much risk: without revealing one's self, sharing one's feelings, accepting one's vulnerability. And all of these things are very difficult to do. The very nature of love, for men, involves a risk of self-revelation. A man must acknowledge to himself, "This is what I feel on the inside and that places me in a vulnerable position. It also means I am not in control."

One of the most frequent ways men often attempt to deal with vulnerability in a relationship is to hide it. However, if they recognize the strength that comes from sharing vulnerability with a woman, they can increase the intimacy level of the relationship with her. But it is difficult.

Risk-taking can be physical ("How fast can your car go on the Autobahn?') or emotional ("I need you'). In a relationship, physical risk-taking can take the form of hugging, kissing, touching, etc. Emotional risk-taking can take the form of sharing feelings, telling the other person about their importance to you, revealing hidden worries, fears, and so on.

All attempts to establish connections between people involve risk. How an individual decides to handle risk has implications for the type of relationship that can develop between people. I will share something that happened to me some years ago to illustrate the power of emotional risk-taking. The words of this man ring in my ears, and to this day I can still picture his face.

I had gone to lunch with John, a counselor in a community mental health center where I was doing my doctoral internship. He had started talking to me more and more, and we were becoming friends. I enjoyed the time we spent together at work as we shared ideas about life, philosophy, and our field.

We were assigned a seminar to conduct and began to plan it. I liked him, looked forward to seeing him, but had no romantic relationship with him. He was not especially handsome—a man of average attractiveness on the outside, most women would probably say—but there was something special about him. I valued him for several reasons, one of which was that he appeared to be a giving person.

After a planning meeting, John and I stopped for lunch at an Italian restaurant. The dining room was somewhat dark, with tablecloths and lighted candles decorating the tables. I wore a royal blue dress, one I especially liked but not anything that would stop a crowd, and he wore regular khaki slacks and a brown-and-white striped cotton shirt. We were both dressed in work clothes and were heading back to the clinic for a full day of seeing patients.

We ordered lunch, the waitress brought the meals, and we were actively involved in conversation. At least, I thought we were. It was me who was involved in conversation. I talked and ate my lunch and said something else and then took another bite of food. Finally, more than halfway through lunch I realized that John had not touched his food. It remained on his plate.

Embarrassed that I had not noticed earlier, my own plate now nearly empty, I tried to say something to salvage my lack of attention to him. "Was there something wrong with your food?"

He smiled, looked at me, and with a very serious expression, the candles reflected in his blue eyes, said, "I'll get the waitress to bring me a doggie bag to take with me back to the office. There's nothing wrong with the food."

He paused and then he said, "In this room with the candle shining on your face and hair, I can't get over how beautiful you are. I have no appetite."

We left then, and on the way back to the office I said very little. I am a verbal person but had nothing to say. On that day, I learned how powerful the sharing of a man's emotional vulnerability could be. I attempted to capture the feeling in a poem.

How to Tame a Woman

Not with force
  or fear
  or control
But with tenderness
And vulnerability—your own.[3]

LOVE AND SELF-AWARENESS

A man who understands love recognizes that a relationship with another person is affected by his relationship with himself. As a result, he tries to continue to grow in the area of self-awareness. This does not mean that he is perfect. It simply means that he is committed to the process of understanding himself as an important part of life. There is, as I have told my students and patients over the years, no substitute for self-awareness. The more I understand myself, the better I am able to problem-solve situations that occur in my life. Self-awareness is a process—a path that thinking people continue to travel in their journey through life.

One of the stories that comes to mind here is that of a colleague of mine, a Scottish psychologist named Tom Williams. Dr. Williams wrote a paper for me that summarized several of the ideas he has tried to put into practice in his personal journey to become a more self-aware person. He takes the position that a man who believes in love is a man who believes in himself. Some of his ideas on self-awareness and his commitment to growing as a person throughout his lifespan are quoted below.

> I have always identified with the quotation by Henry David Thoreau: "If a man does not keep pace with his companions, perhaps it is because he hears a different drummer. Let him step to the music that he hears, however measured or far away."[4]
>
> Exploring the concept of men who believe in love is fundamentally an exploration of men who have come to believe in themselves—some for the first time and some as a familiar place to return to. In looking at my own life, and in those events that taught me to understand who I am, I am struck by the influence of love and of women who, beyond the shadow of a doubt, have consistently been my most powerful allies and teachers. I have entitled my paper *The Role of Women in Showing Me the Way to Believe in Myself* and would like to share some of those ideas here.
>
> I am a native of Scotland, my Ph.D. is from Glasgow University, and I am married and have three children. I have taught in Scotland as well as Australia and hold degrees in science, psychology, education and educational psychology. I love the outdoors, enjoy hiking and find relaxation in T'ai Chi. I also hold qualification in traditional Chinese medicine and have a part-time practice in acupuncture. How did I get to this point in my life? I guess I have always tried to understand myself.
>
> I will share with you one of my experiences. The first area

of self-awareness I was forced to face was something very basic. It had to do with identity itself, and I became aware of this when I was quite young.

At the age of eight I was sent to a famous all-boys' fee-paying school in Glasgow. There I was to learn about what was necessary to become a man and to take my place among the other men who totally surrounded me. Although I was quite unaware of it at the time, the dominant ideology of a patriarchal culture was at work. Its goal was to make sure that I conformed and asked few questions.

Everything at school was competitive—school work, homework, army cadet corps, and above all, sport. To be good at sport—rugby, cricket, athletics, etc.—was to be accepted into the culture in a way that even high academic achievement couldn't touch. There was something about competition at school that raised sport to heights that approached mystical adulation.

To be fair, winning was not always seen as being that important in itself, but to be competitive and combative was all. The shaping of the patriarchy seemed to demand this commitment. And while there was an illusion of individuality and personal choice, there was equally never any doubt as to what was really expected of you.

In this situation I survived and on the face of it, prospered. Academically, I was bright—although by no means as bright as a fair number of my peers—and above all, I was good at sport! If you are good at sport then it is quite amazing how you can ignore your deficiencies and cut off so many channels to personal and psychological growth. It becomes totally outrageous if one ever is in a position to realize it.

Yet, despite the fact that I was succeeding in this system, something inside kept nagging away at me. Something was not right; I was missing something, yet I was never able to put my finger on what it was. The problem was that whenever I got to thinking in these terms, I got depressed and unhappy. Again, I never knew why.

Eventually, I figured out what was wrong. All the

rewards came flooding in for playing the game, fitting into the system, doing the right thing . . . the rewards are on the outside . . . and that drowns out the discontented voice on the inside. The nagging doubt gets bowled over in the rush to be on the winning side. The patriarchal ideology compromises you at every turn—and the vision of something else—a dream you cannot know but just feel in your heart, becomes muddled and in all practical senses, lost.

So I progressed through the storms of adolescence and on towards adulthood, getting better at things and feeling more and more confused about them, and at that point I really began to learn from my interactions with women.

In the story of my life, six women—more than anyone else—helped me break free of ideological straight jackets. In fact, there are many more than six, really, but these six individuals gave of themselves in a manner that helped me believe in love, believe in myself. Each has her own story. These six include a former girlfriend (from whom I learned that I didn't want to be the stereotype she wanted); a first love (from whom I learned about the oppression that women as a whole experience in a patriarchal culture and from whom I learned to trust the strength of love); a Christian woman (from whom I learned the energy and power of love); a co-worker (from whom I learned to trust hope); a student (from whom I learned the power of humility); and my wife (from whom I learned the power of commitment). Each woman, externally, helped facilitate the internal process of self-awareness in me.

Over the years I have come to believe in myself, because— through the medium of the lives of precious and unique women—I have come to really know what love is and to recognize the potential of it in my life as a force for positive change. As a result of what I learned from these women, I can see myself on the inside more clearly.[5]

What did he learn in a larger context? Tom revealed that he learned the following:

1. That to love means not to compromise when real issues are on the table.
2. Increasingly to trust the power and patience of his own inner wisdom, that "feminine" aspect of himself he had for so long rejected.
3. That love is about actions, not just about feelings and words.
4. That love is about having fun, laughing, and bringing overt joy and happiness out into the world in a way that touches people's hearts and minds.
5. That love without humility is hollow.
6. That love brings with it a companion of commitment.

LOVE AND FEAR

Fear is a powerful emotion. It is primal—a biochemical response that allowed primitive caveman to escape the saber-toothed tiger. Fear had survival value and was triggered by the human brain as a response to threat. Fear can still have survival value in human relationships, energizing people to escape from psychological saber-toothed tigers, although it can also bring people closer.

It is often when fear rears its powerful head that men seek the consultation of others: other men, friends, barbers, bartenders, and even drinking companions. And sometimes, they consult doctors.

Men can fear losing love; they may also fear having it. I recall a student who consulted with me several years ago. It was just after I had given a psychology lecture with a male colleague on the topic of love between men and women. I had returned to my office and was putting my books away when a student appeared at the door. We started talking about the lecture and then he asked, "What do you think about love and fear?"

"What do you mean?" I asked, looking at him thoughtfully.

"It seems to me," he said, "that fear often stands in the way of love. At least, that's how I feel. I am very much in love with my girlfriend but at the same time I am frightened about really getting too involved. It's like I am caught in the middle between two strong forces, each pulling the other way."

Brad was a senior in college. He was a bright, talented humanities major. His long-term goal was to be a university faculty member. He considered life with the seriousness of a young man and yet had a playful side that made him very well-liked by his peers. He was aware of a struggle within himself and assumed that there was some path to lead him to the other side.

"How does this fear affect you?" I asked.

He paused a minute, and then he answered, "It makes me run away from her. I am in love with a wonderful woman who is kind and giving. And when she seems to be getting too close to me, I run away. Not actually, just symbolically. I say I have to study, or go out with the guys or spend time alone. And sometimes I pick a fight for no reason. But it's really, I'm afraid of getting too close. And she has done nothing wrong, but I know it hurts her. And I know that this is something about me—it's not about sex or Karen or age. It's about a feeling I don't really understand, but I know it's fear. And I feel bad."

I looked at Brad for a minute or so. He and I had talked several times as he had been a student in some of my courses. Suddenly, he seemed very grown up.

"It sounds like you are ashamed for feeling afraid of love," I said. "Well, I want to say to you that you are not alone. I think sometimes the whole world is afraid of love. It is a thing that is difficult to understand, and it brings with it a sense of futility in trying to hide."

He looked somewhat relieved and then I said this, "Brad, what I think is critical is that you are trying to sort this through. It is your life, and the struggles in each of our lives need to be addressed by each of us. And in facing those struggles, we learn—as one of my former professors would say—what it is to be human."

He and I talked on several other occasions, although he was no longer my student as he had completed all of his psychology courses. He seemed to grow up that year. While I don't think he changed appreciably in height or weight, I think he grew in the respect I had for him.

He received a fellowship to graduate school, got married to Karen, and continued on his journey through life. In time they had two sons. I was simply one person along the way that he learned from, and he was one person who, when I think of him, continually reminds me that the respect I feel for men who grapple with fear is not a function of age. It is a function of courage, as opposed to fear, which is described in the poem below.

River of Fire

the internal river moults white fire.
It runs
wild
and strong
and bleeds
the strength to fight.

It courses
through veins and
pumps hot
into the
gut,
churning.

It brings giants
to their knees
and forces them to flee
the very love
they want.

It is
fear
and it drowns
from
within.[6]

LOVE AND HONOR

Honor is something we don't hear much about these days. I think it was at a zenith during the time of the legendary King Arthur. Honor evokes, for me, images of knights and quests and castles. In a modern world, it is often difficult to overcome the muck of the daily news to salvage a flower called honor. The story selected for this section would scarcely fit into the context of an Arthurian legend. There is, however, a modern hero and man of honor, the loss of honor and the struggle to reclaim it again.

James is a forty-three year old Black American who worked at a café where I would often stop in the morning on my way to work. He was a hard worker, seemed like a kind person and usually had a cheerful attitude. He liked people and enjoyed talking to them in the morning.

He would often talk fondly about his wife and daughter. When he spoke of them, his whole face would light up. It was obvious to the casual observer that this man valued his family. What I didn't expect was that his story would be so amazing.

I asked James if I could interview him for my book, and we spent several hours at the local library, me with pen in hand and him with photos of his life and family. He started off in a way I didn't expect.

"My life has changed a lot in the last ten years," he said. "I guess I should tell you what it was like before." And so he did. Ten years ago he was addicted to drugs. He had spent time in jail for violating the laws related to illegal drugs and for "acting crazy." He had been placed on probation and had to satisfy requirements each week. He had to report to a probation officer and go through drug testing. He said that jail was a negative environment, and he hated what he saw there.

For years I acted out—got drunk, acted wild, didn't have any direction. And then I'd end up in the workhouse (jail) again. The cycle would start all over again.

When I was in the system (jail), I met people who didn't know any different. I saw . . . people who didn't know how to read—grownups who didn't know how to use the law library in jail or how to read mail. I grew up in a small town and this was a shock to me. And the coldness of the system made me a negative person—I learned how to be cold and not care about anyone because that's what the system called for. That's what it teaches you. That's what it taught me, and it doesn't care about you.

The psychological struggle for James involved battles on several fronts. He had to break the self-defeating behavior cycle that repeatedly placed him back in jail. In addition, when faced daily with the cold negativity of the jail, he had to keep emotional softness alive inside him. Such striving is difficult. He continues:

When my mother died, they wouldn't even let me go to her funeral. I was only in jail for drugs—not for hurting people—but I couldn't go. That time in my life was a dark, dark time. It was like a bad dream. And now my life is so much different. That was ten years ago, and now I have a whole new outlook.

How did he reclaim the quality of his life? He regained personal honor.

I changed. Things don't change—you change. When I was given a break, I realized that I had a chance to start over again. So I did. I did what I needed to do. I followed the rules. And I guess it was gradual that I started to make better choices.

What does this have to do with love? When he started making better choices, he picked things that were good for him and allowed himself to be receptive to the caring of others.

And when I met my wife, I realized she was good for me and I chose her, too. We were taking a dental class, and I couldn't get the teeth right. We talked and talked and then went out to get a drink. A week later we moved in together. I wasn't ready to settle down yet, but she was there when I was at the lowest—in trouble. I fell back into drugs. They put me in counseling and I had stricter supervision. It was difficult. They didn't think I'd make it. But my boss believed in me and so did Toni (my wife). They both trusted me.

Remaining open to the caring of others involves a self-worth component. In order to accept another's love, one must feel lovable. James explained the process of reclaiming this feeling about himself:

I think I began to feel worthy of love again when I met Toni. For years I had wasted my life. Then when I met her, I began to feel better about myself. I guess I just lucked out. I had made up my mind to be a bachelor for the rest of my life and then she walked in the door and *bingo*—that was the end of that.

Now I have a job and a family. My little girl Morgan Lozia is two years old, and when I come home from work, it's like a whole new world. My home is a place of comfort. I can play with my daughter. It's like my chalet—I can go there, relax and be happy.

James also accepted honesty as an important component of two relationships: one with himself and one with a woman. His wife provided encouragement but the choice was his.

Toni is someone everybody likes. That helps me. She treats me real good. And it makes it lighter for me, not like being with someone who pulls you down or is sour all the time. Or who tries to hurt you and you have to protect yourself. You can't let your feelings out—let yourself open to get hurt. You have to be macho or cold, show you don't care. But I always did care.

I didn't realize how much I was changing until it had already happened. I think you are basically born nice. I learned how to be contrary. And when I met Toni I saw she was a nice woman. She said, "You don't have to be cool with me." I could trust her even though I didn't at first. And each time something came up, she handled it well. She hung in there with me, and we are good friends.

You see, I learned kind of late in life. I'm lucky to be living and I'm glad I didn't give up. I had to overcome what I was told as a kid—"you're the best"—because I was an only son. All my life my mother protected me; my father protected me; living in my hometown protected me. And I had to learn to handle things myself.

I like my life now. And I don't even mind getting up at 5 AM to go to work or to put the garbage out in the snow. I guess it's that love.

James made reference to relationships that have a positive effect on men. He compares those to ones that hurt men or require them to be emotionally armored. Such sentiments have been echoed by many of the men whose stories fill the pages of this book. The next section is from a young man who reports on the attraction for him of physical relations with women in which there is affection, not just physical involvement. His name is Larry French and he is a thirty-five year old sports photographer who lives in Vermont. He is bright, attractive and single.

LOVE AND SEX

"I really believe that sex without love is empty," Larry explained. "The mind is not involved."

His comments were part of an interview addressing issues of affection and touch in relationships with women. He had much to say.

Tenderness of a touch can show affection but touch by itself is not necessarily a reflection of *feeling*. Touch can be for physical reasons alone—to satisfy physical needs—as opposed to coming from the heart. Affection is not inherent in touch.

I think there is a difference between touch that becomes increasingly heartfelt over a period of time between two people and the satisfaction of animal needs which we certainly all have. But those basic needs are meaningless without affection.

Larry continued. He wanted to differentiate issues of relationship quality.

Touch without affection is limited because there is no joy involved. It's an end, not a means to an end, and if it's just physical, it has no place to go. I'll give you an example. Once climax is achieved, let's say if the people have a physical connection without affection, you might find the person thinking only about himself. (I use *he* because usually it's the males who cause this problem. Women get caught in it and end up fooled and angry.) The man is thinking about what he is doing next—this or that—and it's over and he didn't really care.

Whereas, if the people share touch with affection, it is a connecting force between them. The feelings last because the people care for each other. The caring remains because the man and woman have shared a wonderful experience. In the afterglow, affection and touch continue.

"How do you think this affects a relationship?" I asked. Larry replied,

If there's no affection, you don't have a relationship. Touch with affection is the basic element of a relationship. Often this is why relationships end. People become bored. Sex and touch without affection become boring because after you've had sex with somebody a few times, the lack of meaning in the act pushes people apart. The sex was more important than the person you have had it with.

When it's just a physical thing, once you've had sex, then it becomes boring. The excitement of being with *that* particular person was never really there. You might be physically satisfied but the relationship—if it can be called that—would end because it's just physical. People are hurt that way.

At this point I asked him about men's feelings. He had mentioned some already—boredom, hurt, excitement—and this topic introduces issues of personal self-awareness. Larry said,

I don't think it's quite so cut and dry, but I think caring touch comes from the heart: *real* touch, *real* feelings. Feelings can't be created; they just happen. That's why often a relationship with no sensitivity behind the touch won't succeed. It's not balanced by feelings. The excitement of lovemaking should be in a person's eyes. To see what your partner is feeling can make you feel everything else that much more. If it's going to last, that is where it starts.

There needs to be a connection between the mental and the physical. It makes the package complete. Sex is part of love but love is not always part of sex. And there certainly is a difference between having sex and making love.

I'm an emotional person by nature, and I know when things feel right. A couple of times I have experienced just how good it can be and I know how rare that is. Even momentary experiences of true love are good, although frustrating in their briefness for the person who wants, needs and is able to offer continued affection.

"How did you develop your ideas?" I asked Larry. "It seems like you've given this much thought." Very often, the principles one has as an adult are a function of background as well as experience. He explained:

I grew up in a household where there was no touch and little affection. I had to make a choice early in my life to go one of two ways—towards being a negative person forever or towards the positive understanding of how important touch is. I experienced a house filled with anger and decided that I would have the opposite.

Larry recognized that something was missing in his life. He decided he wanted it and so reports he made a conscious choice to have it. He could have chosen anger. Why didn't he?

Actually, several friends would tell you that I did choose anger for a while. They stuck by me while I shed the angry years. The anger from my younger years colored my whole outlook on myself, other people and the world for awhile. The good part of me was deep inside, buried. The catalyst for change was a woman I really loved who ended up leaving me because I was so negative. And I can't say I blame her. I wouldn't have wanted to be with me, either. But after that I changed my life.

We can accept situations or change them. I focused on change. Life to me without a good relationship is little more than existence, though not all people would agree.

His philosophy?

Life reaches out and touches us in the form of other people. Anyone who doesn't allow himself to feel is missing a lot of what I think life is. Whether or not this ends up being a woman you will love depends on a lot of things: the person, the situation, the timing, the chemistry, the mutual affection, and so on. The key, I think, is to allow yourself to feel—to be passionate about things—to be open. The world comes to life that way. If you choose to let go of anger, you can embrace passion.

When Larry shed his anger, he allowed himself to become more open as a person. At the same time, he realized that by doing so he was also choosing to become more vulnerable.

It is riskier to be vulnerable; one has to be strong. If I give up anger and choose love as a lifestyle, it can make for difficult times. But we hopefully and necessarily become stronger as we move through tough times because there is no other choice. If we choose to avoid our emotions and our sensuality, we deny the essence of who and what we are. I guess my ideas show, frustrating as it is sometimes, that I am not willing to settle for less than I want. The deeper the level of one's sensitivities and intuition, the harder it is to find the people you're completely comfortable with. However, when that happens, the energy between the people is that much stronger, basic, and hopefully more lasting.

Larry's view of sex is relational; not physical. He sees sex and affection as a context for mutual sharing between a man and woman. What he wants is both, and he is not willing to forgo one in order to get the other. He acts on his feelings and personal experience, chooses what fits for him and summarizes,

> There are men and women on this earth. I believe we were put here to be together—to be able to live passionately. To share the joy. Such a lifestyle allows for trust and understanding between two people. When we are open with ourselves, we are open with others, like two mirrors, face-to-face. It can work. It's just difficult to find—but worth it.

To Larry, qualitative issues are more important than quantitative. He values sex in a caring relationship above sex without affection and is willing to wait for what he wants as he takes his feelings seriously. He, like many of the men in this book, also reported on an inner change process with love as a catalyst. The next story involves change from the outside, in location as well as lifestyle. Love often is accompanied by inner and outer elements of change.

LOVE AND CHANGE

"Be prepared," he said. "If you let love into your life, everything will change. That's one thing you need to understand."

The speaker was seated next to me on the airplane. He was from Canada, an architect about fifty years old who was working on a new hospital project. We had been talking about work-related topics, and after I told him I was a psychologist, the conversation took a different turn. With little introduction, we started discussing love.

"I attended a speech once," he said, "and ended up in love with the speaker. I moved to the other side of the country, got married, and now have four kids. I often wonder what my life would have been like if I had missed the lecture."

I smiled. Being vulnerable to love sometimes means that men allow their whole lives to change.

LOVE AND BUSINESS

What about change applied to larger systems? Jack Mendleson, DBA, a member of the management faculty at Radford University in Virginia, addresses this question in a paper entitled *The Man Inside the Power Suit*. Part of his work is quoted here.

What will become of men-who-believe-in-love in the corporation, the government agency, the university? Will they be seen as hopeless romantics, goof-offs, or even sexual harassers? Not necessarily.

Management consultant Rodney Ferris, writing in the prestigious management journal *Organizational Dynamics* in 1988, distinguishes between romantic love and "family love."[7] This family love, he suggests, can be extended to work, so that work-family love can apply to our quasi-family at the job. In fact, potentially, managers could view people who are hired as members of a kind of extended family.

Several companies have done exactly this. A prime example is North American Tool and Die Company in San Leandro, California. The president of the company frequently attends to factory workers, just because their children are in the hospital or because it is their birthday. (This company, incidentally, is very profitable.)

A kind of work-family love not only makes sense but is in some ways superior to other ways of looking at an organization. As Ferris explains, this love involves a feeling of caring for the self as well as others; conveying a sense of belief in both and encouragement to achieve the highest level of which each is capable.

Now, it is important for me to outline what male work-lovers do *not* do.

Clearly, they do not participate in seductive relationships with female co-workers under the guise of caring and friendship. Unfortunately, some men may fool themselves as part of their own "hustle" to win romantic acceptance and sexual favors. Such behavior is sexual harassment. One male friend of mine (call him Ralph) stands out in my memory.

We were both recently divorced and had participated in a divorce recovery group at the time I knew him. Ralph was a very forceful character and used his background from the self-help group, along with his intense personality, to get what he needed (or thought he needed). Women found it difficult to get away from him. Secretaries in his company had especially tough times.

Ralph's position as an engineer meant that he often assigned work to the secretaries. Many of them were insecure in their jobs—since layoffs had occurred frequently—and did not want to offend Ralph when he asked personal questions and invited them to coffee and lunch. If a secretary was single and made the mistake of inviting Ralph to her home after a dinner date, he sometimes refused to leave. Ralph never actually overpowered anyone physically, but the emotional assault seems obvious.

Within a few years both Ralph and I remarried and I moved away. Although I lost contact with Ralph, I feel confident he learned the same lesson that so many of us did during that period. Namely, we men must be clear about our motives and intentions. We must know our own minds and communicate honestly with ourselves and others. Work associations often produce very strong pressure toward intimacy. Work interdependencies, deadlines and long hours increase the pressure. However, the best kind of work-family love is nonsexual and noncoercive.

Work-family love is not about power and greed. In the United States, the typical image of the successful male executive seems to be a man obsessed with both. The image that comes to mind is Gordon Gekko—Michael Douglas" memorable character in the 1987 Twentieth Century Fox movie "Wall Street." He epitomizes the stereotype of the man inside the power suit.

While I believe men like Gekko are in the minority, they certainly do exist (as do women Gekkos). Such men are so focused on winning, gaining power and building empires that they willingly sacrifice honor, friends, family, and sometimes even their own health. Ethics often seem irrelevant to them, and even when the law has a lengthy prison term or a truly punishing fine for misdeeds, potential rewards seem too great for these men to give up. I have always found it interesting to note that many such men have been convicted of serious crimes that were committed *after* they had made millions of dollars.

Work-family love can extend beyond one's own bloodlines into all work relationships. Men-who-believe-in-love like women-who-believe-in-love can *thrive* in the work organization. To do so they simply need to care about the nature of the work as well as its people.[8]

Dr. Mendleson's position here is that organizations can change. They can adopt a kind of win-win model in which the affiliation needs of the individual and the production needs of the company are met simultaneously. And it can work. I know, in fact, of a company that did just that. It belonged to my father.

At one point in his career my father decided he had to make a change. Working in sales for a well-known trucking company, he was spending too much time traveling. He decided to quit the corporation and bought a business, a local moving and storage company. Although he never finished his college degree, he was very successful in business. And he ran the company the way Jack Mendleson described "work-family love." He took care of the people who worked with and for him—emotionally and financially—and when employees experienced problems, he was there to help them. Different times he would stop by people's homes; he helped one man with a crippled child, another with legal difficulties; and he took several under his wing, not so much as a mentor but almost as a brother. By balancing personalities and showing respect for individuals, he managed a successful company and helped employees too. These people he viewed as members of his extended work-family attended the funeral when Dad died. He had been retired nearly twenty years.

SUMMARY

This chapter begins the journey of the rest of the book. The psychological ideas presented here are about men who believe in love—men found in different countries, social classes, occupations and ethnic groups. They share their stories so that others might learn. Some of the main points are summarized below.

1. Men who believe in love recognize loving as part of their identity and make a difference in the world around them by acting on their love.

2. They learn somehow to discriminate between gender and personality in dealing with women. That is, when they experience pain as a result of cruelty from a woman, they are able to understand it as a function of her personality ("she's cruel") instead of something inherent in her gender ("all females are cruel").

3. When they experience love, although they don't always know that's what it is or how to deal with it, they fight the tendency to reject their feelings, dissociate from them or run away. Instead, they stay and, sometimes by consulting with others, work their feelings through so that out of confusion can come understanding and change.

4. When faced with the choice, they choose love. A man who believes in love has the courage to choose what fits for him. In doing so, he reflects a level of self-confidence, belief in himself and timing. Sometimes it takes a while to build up to that psychological point.

5. They accept that love involves risk and they take that risk. Emotional risking and physical risking are both parts of the risk that men take to increase the level of caring in a relationship with a woman.

6. They value self-awareness. They realize that (a) their relationship with themselves can affect their relations with others and (b) self-awareness is a lifelong process.

7. They acknowledge fear, even if it is fear of love. And they act in spite of that, if not initially, once they realize they're afraid.

8. They choose honor, even if doing so may follow a series of mistakes.

9. They differentiate between sex and affection and prefer a combination of both.

10. They accept that change accompanies love.

11. They are different from men who don't believe in love.

2 Men Who Don't Believe in Love

He wore his suffering openly, like a bright-colored jacket thrown over his shoulders for all to see. "I was abused as a child," he had once told her. She had tried to soothe the pain of past injustice with kindness. And she felt such passion for him.

She covered his nude body with fresh petals of red roses and kissed him all over. With a pure heart she loved this man and felt compassion for the sad boy-child she saw reflected in his eyes.

"I love you," he said (sixteen times one Valentine's Day). "And I'm not going anywhere. We can have forever."

She believed him, this man she honestly loved, the one who had said that no one had ever loved him the way she did. And then he left. He sabotaged their relationship, blamed her and was gone. Devastated, she was. He hadn't told her he had chosen to never believe in love.

Emotional pain is seldom as excruciating as that which accompanies the loss of someone we love. It hurts in our heart of hearts. When the loss is unexpected, it hurts even more. The woman in the story above cried and cried. She was unaware that the man who seemed so open to her love had made a decision years before that kept the door of his heart locked.

While there are many reasons men might not believe in love, only some of them will be introduced in this chapter. These ideas are not intended to be all-inclusive. They simply provide a contrast with those of Chapter 1 and the remainder of the book.

SOME REASONS MEN DON'T BELIEVE IN LOVE

---

1. They Don't Choose To.

A love relationship involves the element of free choice. People choose love. Likewise, they may elect not to choose it.

The man in the story had decided years earlier that he would never believe in love. He didn't view it as something real. He didn't think it was anything important. And if he found himself happy in a relationship with a woman, his view of himself within the world would have had to change. He saw himself as someone who was destined to suffer as a way of life. He preferred manipulation to honest love. With love, he had nowhere to hide, and the control he achieved through martyrdom and manipulation would gradually have been lost. For him to have been honest with her, he would have needed to be honest with himself.

In a culture where people have rights, freedom of choice involves the exercise of those rights. Love is simply one thing that can be chosen—or not—depending on the decision of the other person. When the other person is a man, he may exercise his freedom by not choosing love. And while that might be surprising to the woman involved, it is one of his fundamental rights as a person. If he made that decision, perhaps years before meeting her, and tells her that, it will make a big difference. She may be unhappy, but will not feel betrayed.

2. They Don't Realize Believing in Love Is an Option.

He looked at me with huge brown eyes, this adolescent of

sixteen who sat in my office. He scanned the room with intensity and then said, "I am of the generation that no longer believes in love."

"How come?" I asked, wondering what he was thinking.

"Because grown-ups show me that it doesn't work. I mean, look around, once people become grown they stop growing. They act like jerks and lose any ability to relate to people. They turn into zombies that work and sleep and complain in between."

He then took from his notebook two letters. His parents were having extreme marital strife and seldom spoke to each other without screaming. They had no interest in marriage therapy, and Tom came to the community health center because they were tired of his "bad attitude." He was depressed. Despite his superior intelligence, his grades in school were low.

"Here, look at these," he said, handing me the letters. I looked at them, and for the first time in my clinical experience, had an adolescent present to me something I had never seen before. "These are my parents' love letters," he said. "They are kind and feeling. They talk to each other like human beings, but the people who wrote these letters do not live in my house."

He paused, and then he added, "If that is what it means to be a grown up—that I have to turn into some kind of unfeeling zombie—I just don't want it. I don't ever want to lose the part of myself that these letters represent."

There was no way I could get Tom's parents to enter treatment. Everything I tried failed. I did, however, succeed in showing Tom that there were still several adults in his world who had maintained the part of themselves he wanted to hold on to. And in the end, his grades rose, and he unearthed his dream of studying to be a veterinarian.

Some men have no significant adult to give back their lost or stolen hope. As a result, what they understand as the intellectual options available to them are reduced. They see only one choice; love is not real and not something you can hold on to. It is similar to some graffiti my friend Brian saw in the men's room of a local restaurant. It read, "Love's an illusion, pal."

3. They Don't Understand Love and Therefore They Fear It.

I was writing the psychological history of a fifteen-year-old adolescent boy who had been in foster homes for several years after his mother had physically abused him. He had run away from something like twelve homes in a year and a half. I was reviewing this history with him and the events of the different foster placements. After the first eight he complained about something the foster parents had done wrong. These people yelled at him; these were mean to him; these didn't like him, and so on. After the list was finished I realized he had omitted one family.

"You missed one," I said. "What about Family X? Were they mean also?"

He paused, his eyes softened and he looked down. "Oh," he said, "no, they weren't mean. They loved me."

"And you ran away?" I said.

"Yeah."

"How come?" I asked.

"I just couldn't take it—them loving me."

"How come?" I asked.

"It scared me," he said.

Adult men have echoed this same experience. When they met a woman who really loved them, they didn't understand what was happening. They could understand the possibility of rejection, for that had often been the known, but acceptance and love remained the unknown. And there is something about the unknown that evokes terror in the hearts of humans.

What is not known or understood is often feared. When fear is experienced, we withdraw from the situation that arouses the fear. We run away: leave the situation or reject the person we associate the fear with. This is a "flight" response to fear which destroys intimacy. Sometimes, we keep on running in what psychologists call a self-defeating cycle. By avoiding the unknown situation which scares us it never becomes known. The cycle is not broken. Love remains the unknown. Relationships characterized by withdrawal from intimacy remain the known.

4. They Are Stuck Emotionally Somewhere Else.

Different feelings can be experienced at the same time. We can be angry at people and at the same time love them. When people are close to us emotionally, the feelings we have for them can be very complex. Likewise, feelings can act to cancel each other. Intense rage from the past can act to cancel joy in the present. Sorrow or loneliness from an earlier time in one's life can interfere in how one relates to the present. Misery from the past can splash over the events of the present and stain them.

Tony hated his mother. She was a self-centered, manipulative, demanding person. She controlled him in a demeaning way and showed little appreciation for his efforts to please her. Tony was forty-three years old. His relationships with women followed a pattern. He selected women to become involved with who were self-centered, manipulative and demanding. And then he hated them.

Once he became involved with a kind, loving woman. He controlled her in a demeaning way and showed little appreciation for her efforts to please him. In essence, he treated the woman just as his mother treated him. Eventually, he rejected her.

Tony was stuck in rage. He hated his mother but at the same time, failed to see how his rage controlled his relationships with women. And his poor treatment of a kind, loving woman could be explained by a psychological concept called identification with the aggressor. Basically, it means that sometimes a person who is victimized tries to escape the powerlessness of a situation by acting like the aggressor to someone else. In Tony's case, he felt victimized by his demeaning, unappreciative mother, as well as powerless, since sons are initially totally dependent on the mother. He tried to escape those powerless feelings by repeating his mother's cruel behavior, in turn victimizing the kind woman who loved him. The idea is somewhat complex but the effect destructive.

"How can you be so mean to me when I have been so kind to you?" the woman asks.

"Because my rage at another woman is controlling me."

When a man is stuck in rage, it affects how he sees the world and how he sees women. And it is difficult to become unstuck. The emotional pain associated with the original event that hurt him is often very intense. It creates a scar on his heart—like a cattle brand burned into the flesh. It interferes with and even cancels the present.

5. They Are Operating in a Different Stage of Development, and Timing Is an Issue.

"There was a time," he said, "when I would only seduce and reject women. I would not let them get close to me emotionally. I don't know why, but I acted that way for years."

"How long?" she asked.

"About five years," he said.

She said nothing. What she was thinking was how those women were hurt and didn't even have a chance. They were caught in the "acting out" period of his life.

There has been much research on human growth and development. From the time we are infants on, we grow and develop in predictable ways. Adolescence is a time of turmoil, and if we make it through that, we move into adult developmental patterns. Sometimes, we get snagged on a nail in one of the stages and may remain stuck there for years. The man in the conversation above found himself stuck for five years. Others have been stuck for longer periods of time.

Often, midlife crisis reflects those snagged or stuck developmental periods. What we needed to learn at earlier ages—but didn't—comes back to hit us square in the face. When the person is a man, it can force a re-evaluation of the past. Timing, an issue of importance for relationships at each step along life's path, becomes even more critical.

6. They Categorize All Women and Have Distorted Thinking.

I have a friend who is head of the homicide detective unit for a large metropolitan area. He supervises detectives who investigate murders. He told me that in most of the domestic violence murders, he often knows what the male suspects (husbands, boyfriends, lovers, etc.) will tell his detectives before they are interviewed.

Detectives have to piece together the elements of the crime. In more than 98% of the cases, my friend said, when they ask the male suspect what happened that the wife, girlfriend, woman, lover was killed, the answer will often be, "She brought it on herself."

"What did she do?" the detective will ask.

"She did this or that," the man will answer.

"And for that she deserved to die?" the detective might suggest.

"She knew I don't like this or that," the man will frequently say.

This story is a somewhat extreme example of distorted thinking. From research in social psychology, such behavior is called "blaming the victim," a concept of attribution theory, the study of how people explain what happens in their lives. What it means is this. If a man has distorted thinking toward a woman, he will blame her for things that are not her fault. And then he will punish her because he blames her. The ultimate punishment, according to the detective, is that one person kills another and then says, "She had it coming."

The next poem provides a picture of distorted thinking.

How to Break a Person

> *with blows*
> *that break the spirit*
> *and then control*
> *through weakness*
> *caused by you.*[1]

Distorted thinking is thinking that is not clear. Psychologically twisted, it blocks feelings of compassion because one is seeing the distorted image of the other person like a reflection from a funhouse mirror. When a man's thinking is distorted it interferes with love.

Categorizing women interferes, also. If one woman causes a man great pain, he believes that all women will do the same thing. If one attractive woman is cruel, they all are. If one woman is difficult to live with, then all women are. Generalizing from one situation to all others causes problems in seeing the present situation clearly. It increases the level of error in daily life.

One of the fields of modern psychology that addresses issues within this section is called cognitive psychology. It is concerned with how people interpret events. How we think is related to how we act and how we feel. Human beings are complex, and thoughts, feelings and actions are all interrelated. Distorted thinking causes emotional pain and hurtful behavior. The process of change is not an easy one. It is, however, quite possible.

7. They View Love as Irrelevant and Accept Other Power Models.

"If you want a relationship with me," he said, "you need to do things my way."

"What things?" she asked.

"Whatever I say. I'm the boss and what I say goes."

"What about me?" she asked, "What about my thoughts and feelings—and what about love?"

"Look." he replied, "You can be replaced. I have enough money to get whatever I want. So if you don't like it this way, you're free to leave. It's that simple. And don't give me that emotional crap."

She sighed. Somewhere between the beginning and end of the conversation, she watched as the rules were chiseled in stone while he wielded the hammer.

The man in this conversation is clarifying two things. First, he has power over the woman and the relationship; he doesn't view it as shared power. Second, he believes people are disposable and can be replaced. In addition, it is also quite possible that he and the woman adhere to different models of power. When that is the case, relationship conflict often results.

There are many different types of power. Here are some of them.

Types of Power

1. Personal power: power over one's self based on
     competence
     skill
     belief in self

2. Role power: power from a position or role

3. Power over others based on
     coercive power
     power of the victim (martyr role)

4. Affiliative power: the power that comes from having
     people care about you

5. Creative power: the power to imagine, dream, and build

Five different types of power, just to name a few. The power associated with love is considered a type of affiliative power. It comes alive through affiliation or relationships with other people.

If one person in a relationship believes in the primary importance of affiliative power (love) and the other person believes in coercive power (power over others), there is a basic lack of fit in the power models of the people in the relationship. In looking at the issue of men who do not believe in love, let us assume—as in the example above—that the woman believes in love and the man believes in coercive power. Then there is a problem. He would see her model as irrelevant in the big scheme of things, and she would see his model as causing her emotional pain. What is essentially at issue is that the two people have discrepant models of power.

A reference to two discrepant power models is the basis of the next poem.

To Ed

> *I spoke with my eyes*
> *and you did not listen.*
> *I resorted to words*
> *and you did not hear.*
> *I gave of myself*
> *and you did not value.*
> *And now, when I show you silver,*
> *you understand.*
> *I should have been a jeweler.*
> *not a poet.*[2]

Some power models overlap. One can be president of a company (role power); have many friends (affiliative power); and do wood carving (creative power) as a hobby. Some do not. Choosing coercive power (having power over others) often is consistent across relationships. A person who wants to control others often establishes a network of people to control. There is a fit if the other people accept coercive power; there is not if the others accept a different model like democracy or shared power, for example.

The power models people choose may vary over time. Midlife crisis, for example, often involves the review and questioning of power models one chose at an earlier point in life. An executive who got into a position of power by tromping on others may find himself faced with an inner self he doesn't like when his son, upon reaching young adulthood, rejects him. The midlife re-evaluation this triggers in the executive can potentially cause him to reconsider some of his choices because the price in terms of his relationship with his son is too emotionally costly.

Sometimes too for men, experiencing a personal tragedy—unexpected job loss, near-fatal accident or physical illness—can trigger a type of re-evaluation of power models. When this happens, the resulting outcome can be change.

8. They Fake It.

All of us pretend at times. We might pretend we like a gift to protect the feelings of the giver. We may feel self-conscious about not knowing something so we pretend we do. We might appear as if we don't know something when we really do. But these types of pretending are within the normal range of behavior. They are different from pretending in order to cover up malice.

What comes to mind is a clinical example from nearly twenty years ago. I was working in the south in an inpatient clinic for drug addiction, assessing the entering patients, some of whom were there by order of the court. I evaluated one such man who I'll call Herman.

In an evaluation, there are various questions one asks and various psychological information one attempts to elicit. It is a fairly standard routine. Halfway through the evaluation Herman started to cry. And when he did so, I went on with the interview, continuing to ask questions and gather information as tears ran down his face.

He had told me that his wife had died, and the tears appeared after eliciting that information. However, there was something about them that didn't seem to fit; as a result, I had gone on with the interview.

I was trained to consider my own response to a situation as important information and therefore concluded that the reason I had continued with the interview was that there was something wrong with this picture.

So I developed a hypothesis. The hypothesis was this: perhaps what was missing was in the emotional area and could be more closely examined. So I designed a type of question that only someone who had experienced real grief would get correct. And he got it wrong. We then started to gather additional information.

It seems that the wife had died in a car accident. There was reason to think the car had been tampered with. Her family—his in-laws—had sued him for murder. And he was in the clinic in drug-related treatment as part of his court defense strategy.

What had been missing from his psychological assessment was grief that she was dead. The tears were an attempt to present himself as the grieving husband, a distractor from the possible truth of a situation very different from the one he was presenting.

Most members of the treatment staff commented on "Poor Herman, he's devastated that his wife died." I, on the other hand, agreed with the in-laws. This man had resented her, it seemed, for a long time and seemed happy, in my judgement, she was no longer around. The tears were a means to present one picture of himself on the outside that was very different from the real dynamics on the inside. They were also tears of rage. He hated it that his in-laws could even consider suspecting him of murder, much less sue him. And, what's more, it's quite possible that he did it.

There is no court of law in which something like the story I just shared could be used as evidence. And we are not at the point in forensic psychology to make a determination on the basis of scientific test results that would fit with Herman's story. It does not necessarily follow that because one person does not feel grief, he is necessarily guilty of a crime like murder. However, even though this is an extreme example, it illustrates the concept of pretending. Sometimes, when malice is present, one pretends in order to distract others from a fundamental truth that is just the opposite of the way things appear.

I know of men who kiss women they hate in public so that people will say, "What a loving husband so-and-so is." There are men who send flowers to one woman while they are away on a weekend, having an affair with another. There are men who have sex with several women a night, pretending to hurry to a meeting or home while in reality they are hurrying to another bedroom. Pretenders find safety in how things appear.

9. They Hide.

I worked one year on the university faculty with a brilliant young mathematician. He was so intelligent I loved just to hear him talk, and I learned something important from him about some of the ways men hide.

Al was not vulnerable intellectually. He was brilliant and knew most of what was possible to know in his field. He was vulnerable emotionally, however, and I observed that whenever he was afraid, he attacked. As a result, he had a reputation among his colleagues as being objectionable, an unreasonable, difficult character. The truth was that when he was afraid he hid behind verbally attacking—lashing out—and he was so effective at it that no one ever figured out he was afraid. When I told him that I knew he just smiled.

"You're right," he conceded.

"Thanks," I said. "Because what I've learned from you has changed the way I understand men."

Since then I have observed that men hide in a variety of other ways. Sometimes they become so good at hiding that they even hide from themselves. Men can hide behind ideas; behind work; behind external situations like schedules, meetings, times of the year, and so on; behind the needs or feelings of other people; and behind power. They can also hide behind sexuality and seduction as well as behind women. They can become as invisible as they choose, and their actions are not often recognized as hiding. But they are.

Sometimes men hide from love. I know a businessman from India who met an American woman he found attractive. From Day One what he wanted was to have an affair with her, although he didn't tell her that. What he said he wanted was to remarry. What she wanted was to love him. His wife had died a year before, and he presented himself as grieving. The woman was a sensitive sort and adapted her needs to fit his schedule. She thought that, in time, their relationship would grow.

Each time the woman adapted to his needs, each time she changed her schedule to accommodate his moods or the demands of his work schedule, she did so out of respect for his grief. She did this for nearly a year. Finally, she asked him to be there for her emotionally in a way she had never done before, one that would have publicly acknowledged their dating relationship. He responded with rage. He wanted his needs to control the relationship; her needs were unimportant and thus should have no power. And so he rejected her.

The next day she discovered that he had been hiding all along. She asked him if his children knew they were dating. He said his four adult sons didn't know he was seeing anyone. The woman then understood how he had hidden behind his moods and his schedules and kept her from really participating in his life. The real issues were power (he should have it) and greed. The smoke screens were grief and heavy workload (which he himself structured). Because of the woman's compassionate nature, she didn't see beyond what he wanted her to see. His means of hiding had worked.

Human behavior is very complex, and all of us hide on occasion. But there are men who do so as a lifestyle. Only when someone stumbles onto the person beneath the disguise is he seen clearly.

10. They Are Unable to Bond Emotionally.

"I am not able to love," he told her. "A psychiatrist told me once."

"Why is that?" she asked.

"It has something to do with my mother and me. Things that happened in the past," he said. What he didn't say was how cruel he was.

Not all people are able to bond emotionally, although the number who fall statistically within this category is relatively small. In the extreme sense, people in this group have psychological disorders that interfere with maintaining relationships. Sociopaths and serial killers, for example, view people as objects to be exploited, not people to be related to. They are able to act out cruelty toward others because a necessary degree of emotionality is missing within them. They have difficulty relating to others. While they may pretend they understand and possess feelings, to a large degree they don't. Most emotion is outside their range of conscious experience.

Some theories suggest that these individuals were born with

the ability to love and subsequently lost it as a result of early cruelty or trauma. Others suggest that some sort of genetic aberration prevented it from forming correctly. Still others are uncertain of how to explain the complex behavior of individuals who consistently act out cruelty by killing animals and people as unprovoked expressions of rage. This area continues to be one of active research, and its future holds the answers to questions about the whys of cruel behavior that continue to haunt us in the present.

> *the stranger*
>
> *ice eyes he had—*
> *that pock-marked man looking out*
> *from under his hat.*
> *maybe*
> *he killed someone*
> *maybe he only wanted to*
> *but his eyes ran blue cold and his stare*
> *cut wide paths to the soul.*
>
> *we left that place then—*
> *I forced my friend to go.*
> *she went under protest.*
> *those eyes that chill the north wind—*
> *still*
> *they shiver me.*[3]

SUMMARY

The stories in this chapter provide a contrast to those of Chapter 1. Some of the issues associated with individual men who don't believe in love are presented and explained. They are not meant to be all-inclusive but offer a backdrop against which to consider the stories of men who do believe in love.

The book offers understanding as a goal, not relationship solutions. True understanding is empowering. It allows the individual to make informed choices about certain situations. Understanding functions as both a way to control loss (by preventing emotional pain) and strengthen relationships (by helping partners relate better to each other). It is something for which there is no substitute.

Some of the key ideas of the chapter are outlined as follows.

1. Men don't believe in love for many reasons. One is because they don't choose to. Relationships involve an element of volition; they are based on choice. If a man doesn't choose love, he is exercising his right to choose.

2. Sometimes men don't understand that belief in love is an option. Whether through past history, societal or cultural experience or through exposure to others who might have a discouraging influence on the individual, some men do not view hope for love as real.

3. Sometimes men don't understand love and therefore fear it. As a result, they may withdraw from the situation with which they associate fear. In this case, it may be from a relationship with a woman who loves them.

4. Often feelings from the past—intensely negative or positive ones—can cancel out the opportunity of love in the present. Anger at a mother, for example, could be a feeling from the past that could potentially spoil love available in the present. Likewise, unrequited love from the past (obsessing about a first love, for example) could result in the same effect.

5. Timing and development are personal issues that involve a man's relationship with himself. Both can influence any type of relationship he can have with another person.

6. Not all women are cruel. A man who thinks that since one woman hurt him, all will, may be reluctant to risk emotional intimacy with a woman. Likewise, a man who experiences cognitive distortion—sees, for example, women through his own anger—will seldom risk emotional vulnerability.

7. Not all men accept the power that comes with love. They choose other models of power and view love as irrelevant to what is important in their lives.

8. There are men who, when it comes to love, fake it. For a variety of reasons and motives, they cope with relationships by pretending and live by how things appear.

9. There are men who hide from love, some more obviously than others.

10. There are individuals who are unable to bond emotionally, perhaps for a variety of reasons. Some of those are men.

ON A PERSONAL NOTE

Are you deciding to become involved with someone who doesn't believe in love, or are you involved already? Consider the costs compared to the benefits. Apply in personal business a process often used in professional business: cost-benefit analysis. While the costs and benefits may be different (emotional, psychological, sexual, financial, familial, religious, historical), the procedure is similar. Participation in any relationship involves an element of choice and evaluation.

Remember, too, that some people who do not believe in love change; others do not. If a relationship with such a man disintegrates over time (as they often do), remember that the blame rests on things like timing, personal evolution, ignorance, lack of understanding and personal choice. It doesn't mean that you have done anything wrong. Understanding this is empowering and can soften the hurt and disappointment for what might have been.

Also remember that some of the men who started out in Chapter 2 ended up in Chapter 1 because they allowed love to enter their lives—sometimes love that had been given several years earlier. Not all men make this choice; men choose differently, and some are unable.

PART TWO

Understanding Men Who Love

3 *Love Unseen*

Sometimes love is present but does not show. Sometimes, it is in fact invisible. One of the most beautiful sonnets I have read was inspired by love unseen; the woman who was loved by the writer never knew how he felt about her. Here is part of what he wrote.

> *Arver's Sonnet*
>
> *My soul has its secret, my life has its mystery,*
> *An eternal love in a moment conceived,*
> *. . .*
> *. . . And she who made it has never known.*[1]

"Arver's Sonnet" was written more than 150 years ago to celebrate a feeling of love that was kept secret, not observable but alive, living beneath the surface. It brings to mind a more current example that things are not always as they appear. Love can be present but not readily seen.

LOVE AS A SECRET

One of the first patients I ever treated was a young researcher named Frank. He entered my office—a tall, slim, attractive auburn-haired young man with brown eyes—and requested a consultation about relationships. The family he had grown up in was not a happy one; his parents were not very fond of each other. While his career was satisfying, his personal life was not. "I would like to love someone," he said.

There were women he could date and women who liked him, but he was not emotionally very connected to any of the relationships. It was as if something in him had shut down, something that at one time he felt had been open. Eventually we both understood what.

One week when he came to his appointment, he brought his guitar. "I would like to play a song," he said, and with that he proceeded to play and sing one of the most beautiful love songs I have ever heard.

"That's beautiful," I said. "I'm sure Sarah [the woman in the song] liked it very much."

"She never heard it," he said, and with that he described what had happened.

Sarah was a young woman who had loved him at an earlier point in his life. She had given to him freely, genuinely cared about his welfare and had been a loving friend. He thought of her as beautiful and felt passion for her. He had not, however, been emotionally prepared for the impact she had on him. He felt defenseless and overwhelmed by his own feelings for her as well as his own sense of vulnerability. So he broke off the relationship and literally sent her away.

"How long ago was that?" I asked.

"Seven years ago."

"And you never saw her again?"

"No. And I have no way to contact her. She no longer lives in this town—moved away after I broke up with her."

"When did you write this song?" I asked.

"Last night," he said.

Frank's story illustrates one of the elements that makes it difficult to determine whether people believe in love. It depends, sometimes, on when you know them. The way he treated Sarah, it appeared obvious that he did not value love. Seven years later, he was consulting a psychologist and composing love songs to a woman who never even knew he cared for her.

While there is much more to this case story than can be

shared here, Frank's experience might be conceptualized as follows. When he first met Sarah, he was living on his own, working his way through college and dealing with life on a survival, "use-or-be-used" basis. When he met her, she gave to him with an emotional intensity and purity that he knew was honest. It was something he had never experienced before.

However, the anxiety generated in him by this new, unknown feeling and his fear of his own vulnerability were strong. The combination was stronger than the emotional coping skills he had to handle the situation. As a result, and in the eyes of the outside world, he was unable to do anything but reject the person who caused the anxiety.

On the inside, things were somewhat different. The emotional caring he experienced served as a stimulus for an inner sequence of events. Although it took years, he developed in an emotional way that might be thought of as parallel to the stages outlined in moral development research. Essentially, Frank gradually changed from a "use-or-be-used" person to one who was able to experience empathy for others. The changes Frank made were his own; the relationship with Sarah simply served as a stimulus.

One of the most amazing things about Frank's story is the degree to which his love was unseen. A woman entered his life, he sent her away, and years later he is composing love songs about her. If we could ask her about the men in her life she thinks she most deeply touched, we have to wonder whether Frank's name would be on the list.

In matters of the heart, sometimes much remains beneath the surface. Like an iceberg with much of its mass hidden beneath the surface, the extent to which one person touches another's life is not always readily apparent.

HIDDEN LOVE

I remember a conversation I had with my friend Andrew. He and I were colleagues at the university, both psychologists.

After a joint presentation to freshmen and sophomores on understanding relationships between men and women, our conversation turned to love relationships and the experience of first love as we walked back to our offices.

"I remember my first love very clearly," he said. "Her name was Alice, and she was a student in my fifth grade. She sat in the row of desks right by the windows in the seat next to the pencil sharpener."

"What was she like?" I asked.

"She was amazing. She was the only girl on the tag football team, and I can still picture her face. I was hopelessly in love with her."

"What happened to her?" I wondered.

"She was there for sixth grade and then her family moved away."

"What did she think about leaving you?" I asked.

"She never knew I even noticed her."

"What?" I said, somewhat surprised, "Your first love who you remember thirty years later . . . she never knew you noticed her?"

"Yes. I used to go over to the pencil sharpener at least two times a day. And when I did, I tried very hard to ignore her."

"And she never knew you even liked her?"

"That's right," he said. "I tried hard to ignore her because I was in love with her."

"Well, I guess you succeeded."

"Yes," he said. "She moved away and she never knew that I used to daydream about her. She was really something. To this day I can still picture her clearly."

Even for a dynamic, highly effective psychologist, in matters of the heart what is real is not always what is seen.

The environment and the rules for behavior in a fifth-grade classroom make it difficult to express feelings openly. The issues in such an atmosphere are similar to conditions within different cultures that affect the degree of permission men are given to express emotion. Some of these same ideas were expressed by a Scotsman named Blair Currie I interviewed recently. He also described the relationship that exists between the world of nature and love.

LOVE AS AN OUTGROWTH OF EVERYTHING ELSE THAT'S BEAUTIFUL

"We often miss the beauty of the ordinary." The speaker is Blair, 64, who was born and grew up in southwest Scotland and worked in the meat trade all his life. He describes himself as a workingman's philosopher—a philosopher caught within the turmoil of the working class. A perceptive man, he has made an effort over the years to understand situations and people.

Good people seem to stand out, perhaps more so because of the stressful times we live in today. The pressure and uncertainty make it hard: people are all struggling to achieve something, but once they get it they wonder what they've been striving for. In the meantime, they have missed out on some of the simple pleasures of life. It's important to smell the flowers along the way, although not everyone is capable of "smelling the flowers in spring".

His wife of forty years, Christine, is also a native of Scotland. He describes how the culture influenced their courtship and his own personal development.

In Scotland the emotions are still there, only we don't show them as openly. We are more reserved. There is a song written by Robert Burns, the famous Scottish poet, that expresses the sentiment of the average Scot with a certain amount of intelligence. It was written to his wife Jean Armour and the last line goes "There's no' a bonnie bird that sings but 'minds me o' my Jean!" Feelings are somewhat subdued, but romanticism is there.

Burns wrote in the late 1700s and his works gave the common man pride in "The Lallans," which is the lowland Scottish tongue. He wrote in that dialect, identified with the common man and his work was revered in almost every home. He tapped into the imagination of the people and rekindled a tremendous pride in being who they were and gave them an identity. Burns gave the people something to hold on to. As you may know, the history of Scotland involves a legacy of pain, its pride having been lowered by a series of treaties and historic problems with England. Scotland was viewed as the stepchild of England and its people, to a large degree, were looked upon as being semi-barbaric.

Traditionally, Scots didn't show emotions, but as I was growing up some fifty years ago, I remember clearly how during traumatic times—such as lifeboat disaster or coal mine cave-in in which 128 men were trapped underground—those feelings could be sensed deeply. I remember how people held vigil and waited for hours to hear the news of those survivors and how they would sing the words to a familiar hymn in church, "Oh hear us when we call to Thee for those in peril on the sea." There were not many tears to be seen but you could sense intense emotion. Such emotion, it would seem, was very private.

I grew up in a family where certain things weren't talked about, but the feelings were there. Growing up I was always very proud of my Scottish background, but I think it is perhaps a weakness of the Scottish character that we were not able to discuss love in an open manner. I recall my one aunt in the 1930s and when she visited, she had a habit of kissing the children. We hated it; we recoiled from it because we viewed it as an embarrassment, an intrusion on our pride or a violation of our principles. It was just part of *her* personality.

So, on to love. Love is viewed as a fundamental part of nature. The beauty of springtime, the walk along the river path; sitting in a quiet seat somewhere; love as we knew it was perhaps more meaningful in those days because it seemed to be identified with the beauty of the surroundings. Love was identified with the natural world.

Robert Burns' works were about nature and love. In Scotland even though the climate was harsh, and even though times could create a spartan lifestyle, the beauties of the natural surroundings meant more to us. We associated love and nature; nature sort of conditioned our feelings and emotions. Love was just an outgrowth of everything else that's beautiful.

My story? Well, let's see. The young people used to go to the local hall for Scottish country dancing on Tuesdays. The lads would sit on one side and the lassies on the other. I think one of the highlights for young lads, particularly me, was when we had a ladies' choice—when a lady came and picked me to dance. Your heart was overflowing with joy, but you *wouldn't* show such feelings. I can still remember the first time my wife came over and asked me to a ladies'' choice. This is what happened.

My friend and I were very close and in the bravado of youth we had just decided we were never going to get married. Then one night two girls came over to ask us for a ladies' choice. We ended up walking them home; the next night the four of us went to the movies and we both eventually married those girls. We wouldn't change anything because there's no equating to courtship as we knew it. It was wonderful. I know the term carries with it cobwebs and antiquity—but I feel sorry for young people who don't know the joys of courtship as we knew it.

Several elements here are significant. First, love is viewed as natural—an extension of the beauty of the natural world. As such, the assumption is that it exists and is real. Given the natural beauty in this area of the world, the potential for acceptance of love could be enhanced. In addition, the culture supported courtship between young people by providing dances for adolescents in which each gender was free to initiate contact with the other. Young men could seek out women and vice versa in ways that were socially sanctioned. The power involved in initiating a relationship could be shared. Finally, although feelings were not always visible within the culture, they were felt. A part of love was not readily observed.

NONVERBAL ELEMENTS OF LOVE

Additionally, there is a component of unseen love that is not at the verbal level. It is beyond the scope of words.

Some parts of human experience are so intense or so delicate that we are unable to paint them accurately with the palette of language. Very few parents, for example, would say that an understanding of the bond they feel for their children could be accurately captured in a word description of the uniqueness of the child's personality. Words are inadequate for the task.

The elements of love that are beyond language are similar to some physical phenomena that are beyond comprehension to the everyday person. Distances in the solar system, for example, are measured in light-years. But how many people understand the distances so vast they must be measured in astronomical units equal to 6,000,000,000,000 miles? It is, in a sense, something beyond comprehension.

Consequently, attempts to study the nonverbal essence of love or explain it in words often fail. Perhaps this aspect of love is best captured by art. Paintings such as "The Kiss" by Gustav Klimt and "Dance at Bougival" by Auguste Renoir reflect visually that which is not readily explicable in words. The nonverbal aspects of love define human experience of emotion and relationship. And visual art—painting, sculpture, and architecture—provides the mirror.

Philosophy, prose and poetry offer secondary sources of passage into this hidden world. In the following poem by Robert Burns, memories of a lost love from his youth and the nonverbal elements associated with the love they shared have become woven into a central part of his being.

Highland Mary

> *O pale, pale now, those rosy lips,*
> *I aft hae kiss'd sae fondly!*
> *And clos'd for ay the sparkling glance,*
> *That dwalt on me sae kindly!*

And moldering now in silent dust,
That heart that loved me dearly!
But still within my bosom's core
Shall live my Highland Mary.[2]

The material in this book—the stories of the men's lives in each section—is presented as a beginning. Perhaps what is experienced by one man has been known by another. Even if that is not the case, when one man shares with us the experience of his own heart, whether through his writing, a shared intimacy with a friend, or behind the closed doors of a professional office, we can conclude that such an experience for him was real.

When people share inner experiences and listen to the feelings of others or their own memories of feelings as evoked by the stories of others, they grow. And sometimes, what changes is measured in terms of human understanding, even if it occurs in ways unseen.

SUMMARY

Sometimes love is silently hiding. One might miss it altogether and conclude that love is absent. Some ways to identify hidden love more clearly have been summarized below.

1. Things are not always as they appear. Just because a man doesn't openly acknowledge his love and affection for a woman does not mean that love is missing. It might simply be unseen.

2. Love can remain a secret in a man's heart—unknown to the woman he cares for and even to himself. And it might not come into his awareness until years later.

3. Sometimes feelings can be purposely hidden. If a man uses a lot of energy in acting as if he does not care, sometimes that is simply true. He doesn't. However, sometimes the opposite is true. He is pretending because he cares very

much. Handling the situation depends on understanding what is true.

4. An appreciation of the natural state of beauty can accompany or can even strengthen an appreciation of love as "an outgrowth of everything else that's beautiful."

5. There are components of love between people that are beyond words. They fall more within the realm of art than of language.

ON A PERSONAL NOTE

In moments of contemplation or loneliness, pause and reflect on aspects of your life in which memories of love unseen might be hiding. Remember your third-grade love whose shyness was impossible to reach across with words? Wonder what ever happened to so-and-so who touched your heart without ever knowing? Ever etch a love message on an autumn leaf and then blow it into the yard of a childhood love? While printed in invisible ink, such pictures are nonetheless real. They not only capture life; they are strands of its architecture.

the phoenix

plumes glowing from the journey through fire—
   the orange of pain
      black from the dark shadow world
      yellow fear
         white rage
         red shame
            and courage purple

feather the brilliant passionbird of victory.[1]

4 Resilience and Psychological Victory

"That I can love," he said, "is the greatest victory of my life."
He paused, then added thoughtfully, "that I believe in love is
something beyond victory." He continued:

> When I was five, I wanted to die. I hated being in my
> mother's prison of punishment. I went to the playground
> and tried to hang myself on the school merry-go-round. I
> tied a rope around my neck and then around the merry-go-
> round and then ran and pushed. The only thing that hap-
> pened was that I fell off and the merry-go-round stopped.
> As I was lying there on the ground, looking up at the sky, a
> picture of my future came into my mind, kind of like a
> movie. I pictured my life from where I was now and into the
> future—kind of like a videotaped football game that is
> fast-forwarded to the end. Anyhow, when I got to the part
> where I was 16, I saw myself as big and able to leave the
> house. I saw that then they (my parents) could have no more
> control over me. So I picked myself up off the ground and
> went home, knowing that when I was 16 I could walk out
> the front door like I had just pictured in my mind.

The focus of this chapter is conceptual; it is an explanation
of how David overcame the emotional pain inflicted by his
mother to regain his own loving self. As such, this chapter is

somewhat like a trek up a large hill—the climb up can be arduous, but the view from the top is worth it. It is the most difficult one conceptually, and also critical to the remainder of the book. In order to experience the journey to emotional victory of David and other men like him, the reader must continue the conceptual climb, even though it seems steep. It is, however, the only way to see the view from a different level of understanding.

Remember David, whose story was shared at the beginning of Chapter 1? He described being abused as a child by his mother and wanting to die when he was five years old. His personal triumph will be partially explained as this chapter examines the psychological processes used by some individuals who overcome tremendous odds to remain not only alive to their own emotions but also aware, compassionate, and kind. There is, perhaps, no internal phenomenon that places me more in awe.

First, let us review some ideas from the fields of psychology and risk research in which we find some of the paradigms applicable to the experience of David.

PSYCHOLOGY AND RISK RESEARCH

Historically, psychology has attempted to understand and analyze human behavior. Since this is a complex and difficult task, there have been hundreds of theorists who have written about why people do the things they do. Each theory proposes a model that defines the role of heredity (nature), environment (nurture), the interaction between the two and implications for understanding such concepts as individual choice and behavior. Some theories are very complex; others, relatively simple.

I will call upon the ideas of several theories which are relevant to the experience of someone like David. The first comes from my own schooling.

Stresses and Supports

Years ago when I was a student in graduate school one of my professors presented a model of mental health and illness designed by a researcher named Clifford Swenson.[2] The model caught my eye because it was presented as a formula and was simple in design. It was written:

$$\text{Mental health} = f \frac{(\text{supports})}{(\text{stressors})}$$

For us, let's say that mental health equals supports compared to stressors. An individual's mental health could be viewed as a relationship between the stress in the person's life and the supports available to that person. The stress or support can be internal (e.g. poor or good self-esteem), or external (e.g. an abusive or supportive family). Stress and support can affect a person as an individual or as a member of a group.

Most people can accurately describe the most difficult stressors in their lives. Sometimes stressors involve catastrophic illness; sometimes they involve the loss of loved ones through death; sometimes they involve financial reversal, and so on. Stressors can involve physical or psychological abuse; loss; achievement difficulties; divorce, and so on.

Swenson suggests that one way to strengthen mental health is to increase the supports so as to counterbalance the stressors. If someone experienced a trauma (a significant stressor), then a strong support or several strong supports might be needed to buffer the negative impact on the person and provide some sort of psychological or emotional balance.

David's mother was the most significant stressor in his life. She abused him physically and emotionally. She beat him with a belt and with a wooden stick. She screamed shaming insults at him and continued until he broke down. The harm she caused was immense. David's father, who lived in the home, was away much of the time. When he was there, he viewed parenting as the responsibility of his wife.

The main support David had was in the form of his grand-parents, particularly his grandfather who lived in the same town. David said,

> You felt he would never shame you. To him I was something of tremendous value. He treasured me. He came to greet us with excitement. He made me feel he would still love me anyway, regardless of what I did. He wasn't perfect—he had his problems—but a lot of my power came from him.

In addition, David had two teachers—his kindergarten and second grade teachers—who were kind to him and cared about him. The second-grade teacher, he felt, really loved him. Thus she made a difference in his life.

> She tried to help me. I had fallen behind in my schoolwork and she would sit inside at recess and tutor me to catch up. At the end of the year when it was time to leave, she cried. I had never seen a woman cry because she was going to miss me. I didn't understand what it meant, because I was only in second grade, but I knew it was something good. Now I know it meant she loved me. To this day I appreciate her for giving me that.

Risk Research

The modern field of risk research provides a more complete conceptual framework for evaluating the harm of stressors and the positive value of supports. Stressors that increase the risk of harm are called risk factors. They have the potential to pull the person down. Those supports that have the potential to buoy the individual back up are strengthening and serve a protective function.

Risk research explores what happens to people over time. Some of the studies follow individuals throughout their lifespan to determine whether they will break down or remain psychologically healthy. Other studies evaluate the impact of negative events and the progress of the individual in recovery.

With difficulty, such research attempts to answer why a certain human behavior occurs. The difficulty lies in the researcher's ability to measure behavior in a statistically significant way.

It is beyond the scope of this book to review or summarize risk research. To such an end, the reader is directed to academic resources such as those by Anthony & Cohler[3] and Coie, *et al.*[4] However, some relevant concepts as they are evident from the experience of David will be illustrated.

Single case research—such as that shared with the reader within the pages of this text—is the simplest, least rigorous type of research in the scientific hierarchy. However, it is from the experience and case histories of individuals that social scientists often develop hypotheses which lead to further exploration and contribution to the field. Individual stories can provide stepping stones to the development of new theoretical paradigms.

The protective factors of interest to us here are those which involve learning. They are relevant to understanding David. Dr. Norman Garmezy has studied individuals like David.[5] His work addresses how people managed to remain resilient and bounce back from or adapt to traumatic or stressful situations. From it we can increase our understanding of how to strengthen human personality, since the psychological victories of others provide a forum for our own learning.

Let's look at a partial psychological x-ray of how David remained resilient. He explains in his own words, and then a psychological framework is provided. There are research limitations associated with explaining events of the past from the perspective of the present. However, it is possible that his comments will evoke in your mind memories of other individuals you have known who have achieved similar personal victories.

Risk factors
External (outside David's control)

   a. physical and psychological abuse from mother

   b. school achievement problems
   c. poor southern rural area—low educational opportunity and limited understanding of mental health issues
   d. no adults to tell about the abuse
   e. no peers to tell about abuse until age eleven
   f. mental health problem of mother

Internal (within David)

   g. overwhelming feelings of shame, disgrace

Supportive, protective factors
External

   a. supportive people in his life: grandparents, especially grandfather, teachers (kindergarten & grade 2), brother (who was also abused)

Internal

   b. superior intelligence
   c. personal flexibility and openness to change
   d. ability to think abstractly
   e. coping skills—in imagination and mental imagery
   f. social competence (learned how to get along with people and make friends)
   g. developed a sense of mastery through play and use of imagination
   h. used creative problem-solving
   i. realized that it was the parent who was bad, not him (age eleven)

David's Commentary: Risk Factors

As a child I was unhappy. From an early age I realized the level of ignorance of my parents. I was physically traumatized by the beatings—sometimes I was beaten with something like a wooden laundry fork—a large wooden piece of equipment made of hardwood that used to fit into the old-fashioned washing machines. They were made of oak and used to push the laundry through the machine. No matter what happened, whether my brother and I argued over a toy or whether I sneezed at the wrong time, I was beaten. My mother had no opposition—she was the dominant one—and when nobody else was around she would push the limits.

My father felt he had to back her up. I accepted punishment from him because I felt I deserved it. But he didn't need to whip me because I would have listened to him. With her, it was different. She would line up my brother and me and beat us. I could feel his pain and that added to my sadness.

In school I was not able to keep my mind on my subjects because of all of the events at home. Also, I was rather slow at developing the intellectual abilities used in school—I am a musician and probably had a learning disability when I was young that went undetected—and so it was an uphill climb to achieve in school. In addition, my first-grade teacher didn't like me very much because I didn't do well. She complained a lot to my mother, who then beat me. The teacher also ridiculed me in front of the whole class. She never saw any of my problems as her fault. As a result, I was spanked a lot.

I couldn't tell anyone about the abuse because I considered it somehow a disgrace. In the area I grew up, there was a strong bias that children should be quiet and do exactly as grown-ups say. It was awful to keep all of that inside of me. The cumulative impact of all of this was that it lowered my sense of self-esteem and belief in myself. To this day I can remember the pain.

David's Commentary: Protective Factors

I've already told you about my grandfather. Because he loved me and treated me like I was a treasure, I viewed him as the source of my emotional power. And the teachers—my kindergarten teacher and second-grade teacher—both of them cared about me and tried to help me. For that reason they were important because it was such a contrast with how my mother treated me.

David now knows that he is intelligent because he has been formally tested. He also sees himself as creative. His basic self-image as creative was established very young, as he explains.

Because I am a musician, I have always known I had a good imagination and was highly creative. I can picture my name in music and write songs in my head and I always have, since I was eight. I have also been able to accurately visualize things in my mind—in three dimensions, color, and rotate them around in my mind to get a different view. This creative ability—the ability within my mind—helped me to survive and cope with this abuse. My mind was the source of my personal power.

Flexibility

The brain of a musician is flexible—spontaneity was always there as a part of my mind. Because I could think in so many different ways, I adapted easily to change which opened up new possibilities.

Ability to Think Abstractly

In Play
First, when we were young we made most of our toys. We used our creativity to turn something common (like a stick) into something special (like the sword of a knight or the gun of a cowboy). Through play I became accustomed to taking something from everyday life and making it into something abstract. Because I could do this in play, I think I was able to do this in dealing with problems, too.

In Dealing with Problems

At the beginning of this chapter appears David's description of wanting to die at age five. That he considered hanging himself from a merry-go-round is a reflection of both his level of despair and a thinking style equivalent to that of a much older child. Afterward as he lay there on the ground, he pictured his future opening up and at age sixteen being able to leave home. While the suicide component is extreme, the glimmer of hope from the future shining into the present allowed him to tolerate a dark, abusive present. He went home, knowing freedom was around the corner, even if it was a long corner. He had solved the problem in his mind.

In Being Able to Construct Reality in a Symbolic Way within the Mind

Every time I failed or made a mistake, I was physically punished and verbally abused. And while all of this was going on, I'm being brought up in a religious sect that kept telling me how I was supposed to be thinking. In my young mind I disagreed. I didn't see how people who were supposed to be following the Bible could be so very cruel.

Everything about this set me up to be hurt, angry, and victimized but I figured out a way to be a different type of person. I felt I was always wrong in my parents' eyes. What the world shared with me that was supposed to be love was neither rich or alive. It wasn't even beautiful. It was something being presented as real that was not.

In my mind was a different understanding. My imagination was filled with music and vivid colors; it was alive and sexual. And in there lived a secret: that I was good. Something in me looked at what other people thought was love and compared it to what I saw when I looked inside. My inner world of imagination was rich.

The significance of being able to construct reality in a symbolic way within one's mind is this. If a boy is victimized or experiences a chaotic, unfair world, this mental ability provides the tools to make sense of the chaos. As a result, he is able to put some solid mental ground under his own feet which might otherwise be found suspended in mid-air. The unknown becomes somewhat less frightening and the moodiness of a disturbed parent can be somewhat buffered. His mind becomes a source of personal support as well as solace—in this case, within the imagination.

Coping Skills

I had tried to hide from my mother from an early age, and I realized that no matter where I would go, she would find me. And I couldn't win in a battle with my parents because it wasn't a fair fight. So at age eight I started shutting myself up in my room to create. I nourished myself through music—I started writing songs and playing instruments—and the song going on in my head was good enough for me to impress myself and enjoy myself at the same time. And it was this that saved me from the overwhelming sense of shame that was threatening me from all sides.

Fighting back using my music and art was a conscious choice I made at age eight, although parts of this were not at the verbal level. My music and art were just for me, and I believed in them. And I knew they weren't going to hurt anybody. I am motivated by creativity, energy and imagination, not by power, money, religion or authority. And that natural process, pure in its beauty, is filled with power—artistic power, the power to be.

Handling the Pain of Abuse

I kind of pushed the pain into energy and used it as a battery to fuel me. All the feelings they built in me—hatred toward my parents, all the things they did to push me down, to abuse me—all the energy, instead of throwing it back at them as hatred, I took it for myself. I blocked out what they were doing and I stuck with what I wanted. I stayed in my imagination dream world and my dreams grew. They became stronger. The ugliness became music—beautiful music.

The significance of what David did with the pain is this. Essentially, he learned at a young age to recycle emotions—to take hatred and recycle it into energy to fuel his music. While we are advanced as a civilization in being able to recycle organic material such as trees, paper and metal, we are still learning how to do the same with emotion. The physics of measuring emotional energy conversion is primitive, at best. However, this process has tremendous implications for anyone who, having experienced great pain, would like to convert the negativity into some positive process. Case studies such as this one provide some insight into how this might be accomplished.

Social Competence

Because the people in my family didn't treat me well, I had to learn from others how to act. From the time I was young, I observed others. I watched how people outside my family treated each other—how they wanted to be treated—and I copied them. I learned by observing and that's how I made friends. And kids liked me.

Development of a Sense of Personal Mastery

From the time I wanted to die when I was five, I discovered that if I could picture something in my mind, I had the potential to make it come true. When I was able to picture leaving the house at sixteen, I had a sense I could do it. And in the world of imagination, I was always facing a challenge and being successful. Whether I pretended I was an Indian tracking down the deer or a cowboy on the trail of the bad guys, I saw myself being able to be strong and overcome obstacles.

You see, in the world of imagination, I was always in control—in charge. You control the game; you write the song or the play. The result is gratifying.

When I was 10, I decided to face my fear of the dark. I was always afraid of the dark, maybe because I thought there was a boogie man out there or something. Anyhow, one night I woke up and was afraid, so—after getting up the courage—I went down to the kitchen, got a butter knife and called out the dark. "OK," I called out, "if you're out there, come and get me."

Well, nothing happened. So I went back to bed and I haven't been afraid of the dark since. The negative thing (fear) went away when I turned around and stopped running.

Creative Problem-solving

When you make your own toys, you become used to thinking in a variety of different ways. A nail could be transformed into a trigger for a gun or a piece of wood. Discovery comes from necessity. If the right materials aren't available in the physical world, your imagination can make up for that. The way I used my imagination and music as a way of fighting is just one more illustration of how to approach problems creatively.

Attributing Responsibility for the Abuse

When I was eleven, I finally got the courage up to tell someone I had been and was being beaten. I told my friends. I felt a lot of shame but they were sympathetic. "That's abuse," they said. And because they believed me and felt bad for me, I realized that there was something wrong with my mother. My parents had told me that it was right, what they were doing, but I didn't think so. Then when my friends said it wasn't, I realized I was right. I wasn't completely comfortable telling people I was being beaten, but it made me feel better the way my friends responded.

David's Summary

When asked how all of this had affected him, David said this.

The memory of the pain I experienced in my youth is always with me but it doesn't feel now the way it did when I was young. I will never be as vulnerable as when I was five years old. I think in dealing with the emotional pain, part of it I internalized. It forced me to become very strong; my music became an escape. In the world of imagination, I was playing with sounds and rhythms and music. And I also found happiness with other kids. And although I was being punished for certain things, I knew I had talents that gave me a sense of freedom and self-esteem.

For years I denied that my mother existed. Now I don't feel that way. I no longer wish harm to come to her, or anyone. I guess along the way I learned a certain compassion that I needed to learn. And I've seen from experience that compassion works.

I always knew that I would succeed somehow. It has just taken a while. I have not yet found a partner with whom to share my entire life but I would like one. In the meantime I'm sharing with my friends. I express my love with passion through my music which is heard by thousands of people. Though I have felt the strength of passionate love for a woman push and pull within my heart, it is a power within me yet unharnessed.

I believe in love. It is one of the things that gives my life meaning. And I continue to learn more about it as I look for a life partner. I believe as I learn more about love, it will continue to quench the thirst that has parched my lips for many years.

Review and Commentary

Any summary of a story like this takes at least two forms: analysis and emotion. The clinical importance of such a personal experience is displayed in Table 1. While many of the risk factors were *external*, they were balanced by supports that were *internal*. As such, this is a picture of tremendous hope for other men who, like David, experienced intense pain while young. The ability to mobilize internal supports to fight external stressors means that the individual does not have to remain cast as a powerless victim. Internal resources can be developed.

Emotionally, the struggle and victory of David, age thirty-seven, reflects a lifetime of experience. As such, it is difficult to extract factors and say, "This is why he turned out the way

Table 1. David's Psychological Experience

RISK FACTORS (–)	POSITIVE SUPPORTS (+)
External	
abuse by mother	grandfather, teachers, brother
school achievement problems	
cultural ignorance	
l about abuse	
no peers told about abuse until age eleven	
mental health problem of mother	
Internal	
overwhelming shame	superior intelligence
disgrace	personal flexibility
lowered self-esteem	ability to think abstractly
	coping skills
	social competence
	developed sense of mastery
	creative problem-solving
	attribution of abuse to mother, not to worth of self (age eleven)

he did." There are, as mentioned previously, difficulties with explaining things in the past from the perspective of the present. In addition, sorting out the sources of strength is different from searching for strengths within a person. It is hard to separate the factors that affected David at the same time and know how much importance to give each one. Yet his story is instructive in a number of ways.

Human beings are vulnerable to being hurt. To remain emotionally vital, one assumes a certain amount of vulnerability. If one is able to intensely feel love, one is equally vulnerable to feel hurt. The two are parts of the human experience. And there are accumulations of stress that ultimately cause one to break down.

However, we can study individuals like David who have tried to enhance their progress through life in the face of such stressors and learn from some of the ways they succeeded. There are multiple sources of strength people can draw on, both outside themselves as well as inside. David found strength from his grandfather, his teachers, his music, his intelligence and confidence in his abilities.

Sometimes, the most powerful stories of psychological victory remain untold. Such stories may involve psychological recovery from trauma, the journey back from mental illness, overcoming obstacles that crush the human spirit and so on. Psychological victory is often a secret kept within the pages of a personal life journal.

The story shared by David provides some insight into some of the personality-forming power of several types of behavior that worked for him. As such, they might also work for others.

SUMMARY

---

1. Supportive individuals can help to buffer the pain of stressful events. Supportive people are sources of love, self-esteem, and provide an alternate model of what it means to be human. Pay attention to the alternate models.

2. Women who are kind can also provide alternate psychological models to women who are not. Some men, from a young age, can tell the difference. Men who believe in love see women as individuals and maintain a picture in mind of a loving woman.

3. The mind is a powerful tool in shaping an individual's life. It can carve out spheres of safety in the midst of chaos.

4. Maintaining flexibility allows an individual to adapt to negative stressors, which are often unpredictable, without giving up hope.

5. Abstract thinking involves higher-level mental process, which includes picturing events in one's mind to obtain a different perspective. When David pictured the movie of his life, fast-forwarded to age sixteen, he was using abstract thinking. In this case, it gave birth to hope. Seeing the big picture can help when the immediate one is overwhelming.

6. People learn to cope with difficulties by watching other people (observation), by practice (behavior), and by reviewing events in their minds (using mental imagery), among other ways. Each way can be potentially helpful.

7. A sense of mastery is developed when a person feels capable of doing things that are important to him or her. Confidence developed in one area can provide strength for facing obstacles in another.

8. There are many ways to fight. Sometimes, when the situation is unfair, it is helpful to understand that the traditional ways of fighting won't work, and creative approaches might be tried.

9. When David realized that there was something wrong with his mother—and not with him—it freed him from the burden of guilt that is often placed unfairly on a victim. The way people interpret causes (called causal attribution) has tremendous implications for how effectively they problem-solve and what they identify as the problem. Don't

blame yourself for all that goes wrong. Not everyone is able to give love even if you are able to both give and receive it.

10. If you would meet David at a social event, what he has shared from the inside would not be apparent from his outward appearance. He looks like an average person, has an engaging smile, a kind manner, and is very accomplished in his field. He has men friends as well as women friends and people genuinely like him. He tries to help others, is attractive in a traditional sense and shows much emotional intensity when discussing his field of music. He encourages others to develop their own creativity, and he listens.

His experience caused him much pain. That he overcame such personal violence is not a denial of the pain. His victory exists in spite of it. Psychological victory is not obvious from external appearance. It is viewed from inside.

ON A PERSONAL NOTE

There is a part of the story of David inside each psychologically healthy individual. It is the victory achieved by what we refer to as the essence of human nature—the strength of the human spirit—the part of all of us that persists in the face of overwhelming adversity. Seldom are the details of such dramas shared but they exist in different forms in each of us. Analyzing how they work is often as difficult as describing the light refraction of a sunset. However, we can each savor the beauty and at the same time respect the phenomenon. I encourage you to acknowledge your own inner victories. Seeing them is part of maintaining self-respect.

5 *Men of Love in a World of Violence*

"I and many other African American males," Floyd said, "share the experience of going back to our homes, only to discover that we are the only ones to have survived. All the others with whom we grew up are either dead or in jail."

The speaker is 32 years old, the Reverend Floyd Thompkins, Jr., Assistant Dean of the Chapel at Stanford University. I heard him speak when he was at Princeton University and have kept in touch with him ever since. He is a self-directed individual who has dedicated much of his life energy towards fighting racism, ignorance and educational mediocrity. At present, he directs a program that has successfully reduced virtually all of the violence in a high school among the adolescents in the target group. A theologian who has written a paper on the topic of Ebony warriors of love, Floyd is a man of love in a world of violence who has made a difference and someone for whom I feel tremendous respect.

> In working with these young men, we had to deal with the issue of helping them feel safe. Their reaction to not feeling safe was to have others join them in violence. They felt nobody was on their side. No one was concerned with their safety. Everyone has to have someone in his/her life who broods about issues of safety and intervenes when necessary. My parents did that for me. They intentionally did not tell me when I was in danger. They simply intervened to make sure I would be ok.

I was the first African American to enter an all-white elementary school in Bointon Beach, Florida. The year was 1968–69. My mother had to fight the crossing guard so that I would be kept safe from cars. I didn't understand that there was resistance to my entering school—I was only five—and I never felt unsafe enough that I felt violent within me so as to make violence happen on the outside of me. My parents were older and took their responsibility very seriously. They never told me I was poor, and I never thought I was unsafe. Therefore, I was able to risk love and relationship in a way that was different. And people who are able to risk that do better. For Black kids to risk making friends across other group lines takes an amount of courage, but I didn't know that. My parents made love a normal and acceptable way to be, and it was assumed I would have white friends.

My father worked all his life as a train station porter, and my mother worked as a barber. Both of them were an adult presence who said, "You're right in what you're doing. Keep risking." So we did.

Floyd was raised with a sense of self-efficacy—a sense that he could succeed in the tasks he faced. His parents provided emotional support and psychological modeling. They conveyed that they believed in him and in the importance of the issues they were facing. He continues:

They always encouraged me to look at what I could do—to problem-solve. And I do that with the young people I work with. There is a fundamental concept of empowerment that suggests that "You can make a difference. You are an actor on a world stage, and you can help the outcome." That concept makes a difference in people's lives.

Because these were violent times, Floyd faced overt issues of racism and violence. His parents attributed the cause of the problem to racism (something outside the person). As a result, Floyd was prevented from internalizing the shame associated with the rejection of one race by another.

There were friends of mine who died at the hands of the Ku

Klux Klan just because they were African American. These were people I loved who died as a result of violence, ignorance and racism. And when these things happened at each point in my life, my parents would respond, "That's just America." And then they would tell me that there was a need for ethnic education—that racism was the foe and the problem to be addressed. That something needed to be changed and I could help in that process. And I have tried and continue to do so.

The best things to give a child, I think, are passionate parents—ones who feel deeply about something—and a clear philosophy and theology. I never felt I was living in chaos. I was taught to look at both how the world is and how it could be. And I was given the expectation to "make the world better." That expectation, I think, helps people strengthen character.

How can we get more people to fight cultural problems instead of each other? One way is to share the stories of men of love in a world of violence.

THE EBONY WARRIORS OF LOVE

Reverend Thompkins has expressed his philosophy in a paper entitled, *Enemies of the Ebony Warriors of Love*. Some of his ideas are summarized below.

There is a certain kind of person who, despite all evidence to the contrary, absolutely believes that he or she can make a difference. These people audaciously declare that the world is not a fait accompli, rather it is a growing and changing environment. They are driven by what we may call passion, conviction or idealism, but the reality is that such individuals are driven by love. They simply believe that the powerful emotions of sincerity, desire, compassion and caring are undeniable forces in and of themselves. I think of such people as the warriors of love.

When such people cease to dream a world full of truth, love will have died. Only romantic infatuation, lust and codependency will remain. Only then will the world, and we who are in it, be truly abandoned. All will be lost.

There are, however, enemies of those who fight to make things better, enemies of the warriors of love. I believe sentimentality—the quality or state of being governed by feelings, sensibilities and emotional idealism—is what supports and sustains those who would dare to truly change the world. In the warfare between these two forces—the forces of sentimentality and its enemies—hangs the fate of our world, our lives and our humanity.

Before discussing the three enemies of love, I need to distinguish between two types of revolutionaries: those of the mind and those of the heart. Revolutionaries of the mind include theorists, political activists, professional dreamers and schemers who manipulate power. They are apt to modify their individual actions based upon the achievement of greater results.

Revolutionaries of the heart are people who are not methodical, but have a plan to change the world by the sheer force of their own solitary actions. They tend to act on faith.

These two types of revolutionaries are not exclusive to one another, but they are distinctive in their ideal of sentimentality. Revolutionaries of the mind manipulate sentiment; revolutionaries of the heart are captive to it.

Love is born out of gratitude for being loved. It is an awakening sense of obligation and the miracle of one's own capacity to make a promise to another. No one invents love or discovers love. Love discovers us. It demands that a person relax internal defenses to believe in a power or goodness beyond the self. It is to be vulnerable by choice.

To be a warrior of love is to be vulnerable to the world by choice and therefore potentially open to attack from the three enemies of love.

Egoism
Protecting oneself, having to be in total control of all the

elements of life and always guarding against the loss of something—egoism—is antithetic to the enterprise of loving or changing the world. Yet this is the way I and many other men are socialized to live our lives. For African American males, egoism is self-protection. It is the forced position of defense. Even if one wanted to be different, one is reminded of the necessity to protect oneself. On the campus of Princeton University, my dark skin stretched across my male body, makes police drive more slowly and ask me if I belong. In Bensenhurst, in what was perhaps the most racially identifiable event before the Rodney King riots, a young man's hue made him pay the price of death.

Time after time behind the closed doors of my office, engineers, doctors, lawyers, custodians, gardeners and psychiatrists have admitted to me that they yearn to believe in love, but everything in our world tells them not to. The power of love is in doubt and cannot be trusted. Our relationships all tell us that it cannot work.

At Stanford and Princeton, I have talked to many an African American mother who cannot understand her son's anger and disillusionment in these private, elite schools. I have talked to many a black son on these campuses who have come face-to-face with the awful realization that neither their giftedness, their economic privilege with respect to the African American community as a whole, or their educational attainment excuses them from the plight of African American manhood in America. Some recede to the insulation of egoism, others to the torture of self-hatred and insecurity and still others to a mean-spirited prejudice against whites. Most of us do not stay in these behavioral states, but all of us have certainly visited these cells of human pain.

Even though we have love in our lives, we are under attack by egoism which compels us to withdraw and give up hope—for others as well as ourselves.

Passionlessness

African American men are besieged by passionlessness. We are not dispassionate. We are, rather, seized by passionlessness.

Despair, hopelessness and deep wounds from past hurts define the attack of passionlessness. Men are brutalized by passionlessness.

Most of my childhood brothers, with whom I played in the field aside my house, are now dead or in jail. I know that all of them are just like me. Their strengths and weaknesses are equal to mine. Watching my brothers being brutalized has threatened to destroy my passion and heightened my sense of outrage and anger.

Anger is a dangerous emotion and a consuming fire. Rage is even more destructive. They masquerade as passion while being only a more active expression of frustration than tears. Anger and rage are almost never redemptive. They are almost never passive. They are simply unshed tears and muted screams that evidence themselves as shouts. Because I have worked with those who are supposed to have committed the most passionate of crimes—date rapists—I am no longer easily fooled by passionlessness masquerading as passion.

Neither love nor real revolution can be an outgrowth of anger. Brutality and sensuality can not exist together. One of them is a lie. Passionlessness seductively assures us that love is not only inadvisable but that it is impossible. It portrays love's antithesis—hatred and violence—as the only option.

Cynicism

Love's greatest enemy is cynicism. Its power lies in the fact that it makes sense. The optimism that love requires does not make sense.

A justification for a lack of hope, a mandate to not forgive and a reason to predict that humanity will never rise above the level of its weakness are easy to come by. Cynicism is based on the absolute facts of the world. Optimism requires one to accept a supposition difficult to affirm—that the facts are not always the truth. The leap between a factual world full of skepticism and cynicism and a truthful world full of optimism and vision is an exercise of faith.

With the facts about the African American males' existence so clear, the presence of cynicism in our community is not surprising. Self-doubt, self-destruction by drugs, both legal and illegal, and self-denunciation are the natural elements of having one's existence so devalued. In the face of these chilling realities, it is unexplainable that Black men can continue to believe in the power of love, be optimistic about their own lives, the lives of their loved ones, or the strengthening and growing justice in the world.

The phenomenon of an African American son emerging into puberty only to lash out against his single mother for a father who is not present is not uncommon or unusual. It is just that these young men, so unfamiliar with their needs and desires, have not yet mastered the more subtle and less obtrusive ways of loving Black women—desperately and contemptuously. Males in other cultures in America love just as desperately and as contemptuously. Most of us ask too much of our sisters and require too little of our brothers.

Egoism, passionless and cynicism have taken their toll on every brotherhood. Lovers are battle weary but love is as fresh, exciting and powerful as it has always been. Perhaps the very struggle to maintain love creates its enduring power. It is a gift that is always threatened. Love is the sturdiest and strongest thing in the universe yet it must be treated as most precious and fragile.

Love is, for Ebony warriors and a technicolored army, meant to change the world through the most ridiculous of sentiment and the most noble of aims.[1]

Commentary

Inquiring, powerful minds see a new perspective to an old problem. We seek their views to open our own minds.

One of the most striking elements of the Reverend Thompkins' writing is his ability to do just this. In contrast to the gross ignorance and malice of racism which hurt him and his classmates, he addresses the sources of violence he witnessed. He whittles down what he identifies as the elements that undermine positive forces within people and asks the reader to contemplate and consider countering these. The outcome within the reader is a nonviolent model of problem-solving, which spills over into relationships with others. The tone is optimistic, and the keystone is based on faith. Faith, in this case, that the reader may do just what the writer suggests—consider the impact of egoism, passionlessness and cynicism and balance them with belief in love. And accept the premise that truth lies somewhere beyond fact between optimism and vision. Truth involves a component of faith.

Men who believe in love are leaders who lead in a variety of ways. Some lead by example from center stage; others lead from a position of integrity within the self which draws others to them. Still others lead quietly, from within. They are directed by principles, standards, codes of ethics and belief systems that draw on higher-level process. Often utilizing a type of power different from that which is coercive, they present a model which, when we are exposed to it, we might not initially understand because it is new.

We are accustomed to the stereotyped models of male power—the John Wayne cowboy, for example, riding over the hill with guns blazing. It is often a new experience to recognize as strong an individual who teaches a culture to read or who changes the landscape with the power of ideas. Such experiences are still new and because they have to carve out a base of familiarity in the mind of the observer, their newness creates something called cognitive dissonance. That is, the person cannot readily accept what is real. The mind attempts to reject it, saying, "No, that cannot be." After a while, the newness is accepted and an alternate model can be accepted with the same status as an old model.

I was in graduate school the first time I recognized this dissonance in my own life. It was presented to me in the form of my major advisor. Because he was easygoing and listened to graduate students, I assumed he was weak. I was wrong. In the course of three years I had restructured my paradigm of what it meant for a man to be strong. It meant he was strong enough to be kind and secure enough not to be dogmatic and controlling. That he listened to different ideas was a reflection of his own scientific training and his desire to make the university a better place.

As cultures change, some men of love may be on the cutting edge, leading the revolutions of the heart, as Floyd calls them. Others may be leading from the sidelines. Still others may be involved in battles of their own or in the process of evolving. In any event, they are often fighting violence.

Inner and Outer Violence

There are many types of violence. What they have in common is that they cause injury or harm. Violence hurts people, sometimes from the outside, like terrorism or racism, and sometimes from within, like the psychological violence that accompanies alcoholism, low self-esteem, self-denigration and the struggle to overcome the influence of culture or personal history in order to evolve. The battles associated with outer violence are witnessed by the public. Those experienced in inner violence are witnessed only by the self.

The experience of emotional pain is a personal matter. Likewise, the depth of hurt and loss an individual experiences is often only known to the self. Grief, sadness, loneliness, fear, anxiety, betrayal: such feelings can hang in the air and poison the positive life that struggles to grow. Compassion from others serves as a bridge to understanding some of that intensity; the impact of events, however, is unique to the one involved.

Years ago in my work in the schools, I saw two children deal the same way with grief and loss of a loved one. Two kindergarten children—at two different schools—threw themselves on the floor and screamed in response to a death. The one had lost a grandmother; the other, a hamster. They did not know each other and had no way of modeling each other. Loss of a love is intense and real, even if the event precipitating that loss differs. Add to this picture death through violence—a father killed by a motorcycle gang (as happened to one child I treated), or random violence that left a family member maimed—and you have another, very personal response to emotion.

The tears cried for the death of a loved one are as real to a child as those cried for the loss of hope for the future. Being ridiculed—for example, being called "ugly", "dumb" or "fat"—causes the pain of emotional violence. Whether that violence comes from the world or within the self, the tears are just as genuine. Ultimately, the pain of self-denigration ("I'm so ugly, I hate me" or "I'm bad. I don't deserve to live") can result in self-mutilation or attempts at suicide. Emotional pain caused by violence hurts the heart of a child and that of an adult.

SUBSTANCE ABUSE, IDENTITY AND INTIMACY ISSUES IN MEN

Over the years the nature of my work has allowed me to share in the pain of many individuals. Some of them were patients; others were colleagues. From them I have learned much about the inner process of fighting emotional pain and inner violence.

One colleague I have learned from is an American psychiatrist. He shared the story of his own struggle to evolve. It included a battle with no external foe but one against the world of inner violence associated with substance abuse. A dynamic psychiatrist, Dr. Phil Torrance is one of the most competent individuals I have ever seen in this field. When we worked together in an inpatient hospital I marveled at the effectiveness with which he was able to help some very difficult psychiatric patients. He is also my friend and someone I respect highly. His story of inner war has been shared in this book so that others may benefit.

My father died before he died. He lived and died an alcoholic, most of his life spent in Akron, Ohio, where Alcoholics Anonymous began the year I was born. He never went to an AA meeting; he never acknowledged to anyone—most importantly himself—that he was an alcoholic, and he carried to the end the loneliness and despair of trying to keep secret the progressive deterioration obvious to all who met him.

I am an alcoholic. I existed as an active alcoholic for the early part of my life, and have lived, sober, and grateful to AA for my sobriety, for the remainder of it. These two identities exist within me—alcoholic and sober—and reflect a key issue within substance abuse for men.

What is an identity and how do you get one? I never knew the answer to that because in a dysfunctional family what does seem clear is that no one in the family has any consistent idea of who they are or how to find out. Each day brings dread. Like many men, I was recovering from the macho past, freed by, among other things, the Women's Movement to put feeling with thought and action to reassemble life and meaning.

I never knew what to expect from life. That is what growing up with an alcoholic is like. I never knew what my father's state of mind would be from one day, or one hour, to the next. He was not physically abusive. He never treated me any worse than he treated himself. But I never knew what was coming next. Praise, criticism, angry and sarcastic outbursts, drunken behavior, shaming and embarrassing, affectionate hugs, whiskey breath and stumbling blackouts, driving home so drunk he couldn't walk, the next day taking me with him to visit friends as if nothing had happened . . . all of these were part of my early life.

Wanting desperately to please others and be accepted by one and all, he'd readily say, "I love you" right after he had gotten drunk, thrown something, screamed, and promised never to do it again. "I'll quit tomorrow," he'd say, adding that he didn't mean any harm. All these things he believed as he said them but I said to myself, "If he really loved us he wouldn't do this." Well, I know better now. But the way I looked at it, the only man I lived with, and the only model I had apparently lied every time he said he loved anyone.

Watch little boys with their fathers. Holding hands, wanting to use the hammer, too, swaggering into the bathroom pretending to shave (my grandmother, who raised me in early childhood, caught me once pretending to cut myself and saying "Goddammit, Goddammit, Goddammit'), having a drink of "coffee just like Dad" (a lot of milk, a little coffee). We copy those we love, or come to love and copy those we fear. Sometimes it's hard to tell the difference.

I learned my social skills by watching others. *[Editor's note: remember how David did this also?]* Kids from dysfunctional families are the nomads of the neighborhood, searching for a home at other people's houses and hungrily sucking up any crumbs of caring and consistency shared at the dinner table of friends. An alcoholic parent sets an inconsistent example so the child ends up not knowing what normal is.

My intellectual identity was a shield and a mask, separate from how I really felt inside, until recovery. In my personal side, there were always issues to address. The insecurity on the inside was the other side of the competent, intellectual outside. Here, on the inside, there was nowhere to hide. There were no clear guidelines and no book of instructions. Here there were no healthy male role models, no resources to help me learn as an adult what was missed as a child. Here it was lonely.

"Climb a mountain, drink a beer, be a man." Alcoholics Anonymous has taught me to learn to define myself in other ways. What I am aware of is the impelling wish to fit in with the guys—to be seen as and thus to feel like—a man. I tried desperately to prove my manhood by "holding my liquor." Only since I have become sober have I really noticed the constant bombardment of alcohol messages that men receive: television beer advertisements showing young, sexy people at the bar, movies showing the hard-drinking gunslinger who is the master of every situation.

So where does this all lead? I had to face things within myself I had always avoided. I had to stand when I wanted to flee. I had to embrace a sad, lonely, and, for all practical purposes, fatherless little boy. I was forced to accept my vulnerabilities and do something I had never done before: learn from them. The program of Alcoholics Anonymous, the professionals, friends and family involved in my recovery would provide the text of a book itself. What has been given to me, I have given to others; what I learned to help myself, I have used in my work with alcoholic patients and their families.

My relationship with my wife is much different from my father's marriage. My relationship with my children is characterized by love and warmth. I listen to them and enjoy spending time with them, and they know I love them—not because I tell them with words but because I have accepted into my identity as a man, my own loving self.

The legacy of sadness passed down from father to son in my family—from my grandfather to my father to me—has ended. What I have tried to give my children in place of sadness is a sense of love. While I was an active alcoholic, I was unable to sustain intimacy. And now, although I'm not perfect and never will be, I am able to love.

Commentary

Dr. Torrance realized at a young age that something important was missing in his family. What it was, he wasn't sure. However, he felt the lack inside. Alcoholism was not as widely understood then as it is today, and the influence of family dysfunction on a child's development was not the subject of the extensive research evident today. However, children experience emotions intensely, and bright children often remember painful situations with total recall—the sights and sounds and feelings are pictured like scenes from a movie. The positive situations that are missing and the negative ones that are present have formative impact on the child's developing sense of self.

Initially, Phil followed in his father's footsteps just as the father had followed in his grandfather's alcoholic footsteps. The psychological modeling process, whether based in love or in fear, was strong and there were no other male models available for him to copy. In addition, the disease component of substance abuse accounts for part of the heritability factor. Both physiological and psychological factors are involved in substance abuse patterns of behavior that cross generation lines.

The supportive factors for Phil involved Alcoholics Anonymous, professional staff and family support. In addition, he was insightful enough to determine that in order to break the cycle of substance abuse, he would have to do something he had not done in the past: learn from his mistakes. Such learning involved three parts: (1) filling in those parts of his identity that were incomplete and had been so since childhood; (2) not coping with stress through abusing substances; and (3) acquiring effective ways to deal with stress and inner feelings. Because he persisted, he was successful.

In addition, he describes how along the way he learned to symbolically reach down to the fatherless child part of his identity and provide him love. In a sense, Phil learned to become an emotional father to the child component of his own personality which had longed for his father's love. Once he was able to do this, he was able to provide the loving father role for his own children. As such, this psychological process ended the inner war of alcoholism and psychological abandonment.

Violence within people is different from that which comes from outside. There is no casualty list, and the emotional cost is not as visible as bruises or broken bones. Losses associated with psychological violence are measured by indices like lost joy, peace of mind, inner confidence and hope. They show up in the sad, haunting eyes of children whose families show more rejection than acceptance and in recurrent nightmares from which it seems difficult to awaken. Inner violence often bleeds the strength to fight, for it reinforces a negative self-image, potentially victimizing the individual a second time. And because inner violence is not readily observable, inner victory isn't either. Such stories are often shared only with others with whom one has achieved a high level of personal intimacy.

FEELING WORTHY OF LOVE

Romeo Garcia's is another story of inner struggle. His focus is on learning to feel entitled to love and the happiness that accompanies it. Feeling worthy of love often involves winning a battle of self-esteem within the inner chambers of the self.

Hispanic and a native of Texas, he worked with members of his family doing farm labor when he was young. He has known poverty and has been a hard worker all his life. A graduate civil engineer, he recently received his master's degree in public administration. The importance of formal education has always been something he has believed in, for it has made a difference in his life. Romeo's ideas presented here relate to an education of a different type.

When I was eighteen years old a college professor asked us, "What is love?" I didn't know. I think I had always confused it with other things. Understanding how to love has been an inner battle I have struggled with much of my life.

My ex-wife once told me that she thought I loved myself more than I loved her. And while I have never been very good at responding to criticism from my ex-wife, I wonder if it was actually that I loved my wife only as much as I loved myself (which for most of my life wasn't very much). I was insensitive to her because I was insensitive to myself.

Participation in counseling and reading self-help books taught me that I was definitely unaware of my ex-wife's needs. I simply did not know how to love my wife, which was a result of not knowing how to love myself.

For example, some years ago my ex-wife, her sister, my two children and I were having a meal at Hardee's Restaurant. My wife (we were married then) expressed an interest in purchasing a Hardee's coffee mug to which I responded that we had enough cups and it wasn't necessary to spend the money. I would not have bought the cup for myself and I fully expected her to understand. However, that didn't change the fact that my wife's feelings were deeply hurt, as she would have viewed it as a gesture of affection.

There are many things that I would like to buy for myself but I wouldn't do so to save money (more so in years past than in the present). I wanted to buy nice jeans for myself but instead would buy the lower-cost jeans. But I didn't buy something for myself before buying it for my wife. Because I did not know how to take care of myself, I certainly did not know how to take care of my wife.

Now I don't mean to imply that people who buy the lowest cost items do not have love for themselves. I think it's ok to be prudent, thrifty and practical. Neither does it mean that I didn't love my wife, because I loved her the best way I knew how. I believe it means that I need to know how to love myself before I can love others.

Here is another example that comes to mind about the lack of love I conveyed to others based on the limited love I had for myself. During my first twelve years of public schooling, I was only absent from school for a total of five or six times. For several years, in fact, I had perfect attendance. Now it's not that my health was all that good; I went to school anyway because I didn't feel worthy of staying home when sick. In more recent years the same pattern held true. Over the past fifteen years of employment I had accumulated 800 hours of sick leave. Time was not taken to recover from my illnesses, and this same lack of care I projected onto my wife.

Once my wife had a very painful migraine headache, and I was dumb enough and insensitive enough to ask her if she could nevertheless stay home by herself with the kids while I proceeded to attend a meeting. I later understood that I should have volunteered to stay home, recognizing her condition in the name of love and concern for her. Did I even think of it? No. Because I would have denied my own physical pain, I expected her to do the same. Now, years later, I have a better understanding that in the interest of love it is necessary to learn how to listen and pay attention to what the other one is saying.

How did I change? Historically, there have been several changes in my life. The first involved my recovery from smoking and alcoholism. That happened when I was twenty-six. At the same time I became a Christian. I made a conscious decision to improve my life and I did. Shortly after that I got married. Seeing that Christ loved me gave me a different view of myself and served as a turning point in my life.

The second change came after a low point—when my wife of seven years left. As a result, I started on a mission to understand love and my ex-wife better. What happened was that I got to know myself better. Again, I turned to God to discover the meaning of love. Through counseling, self-help literature and studying the Bible I gained understanding— the deepest of which came from a better awareness of the extent to which Christ loved me.

Unconditional love was something unknown to me and something that for the first time in my life, I came to understand. Seeing how fully God loved me helped me to behave differently toward myself, my family and my friends.

I never believed I was capable of behaving in the loving manner which I have shown the past five years. I have done kindnesses I would never before have thought of and have been able to set aside my own emotions to listen fully to others. And I have continued to try to grow, something I plan to do the rest of my life. There is much yet to learn.

Commentary

There are different life experiences which can, in the course of one's journey, result in a paradigm shift so that the way we look at something changes. Experience within the family, formal education, experience within the world—all have the potential for altering our ideas which then affect our behavior. Romeo's story revolves around the role of religion in bringing about a major shift in his understanding of love.

Acceptance and caring combined with a worldview that

gave him a sense of self-acceptance from a power greater than himself changed his view of himself. He felt more lovable and thus was able to be more loving. What he learned from his therapy and his self-help books he was able to apply in a fuller context because his picture of himself had changed.

Self-acceptance increases one's sense of empowerment. Romeo's concluding comments reflected that he was now able to act in loving ways which he never thought possible for himself. His sense of self-efficacy ("I can do it") had increased; personal power was strengthened; and he has continued his commitment to grow.

Resources affect people differently. Remember David from Chapter 4? Religion served as a source of discrepancy for him—a way his mother covered over the child abuse she conducted on her sons. It is not, then, the presence or absence of a particular potential support that makes the difference for the individual. What is often decisive is the qualitative impact on the life of the person. Romeo's church gave him a deeper understanding of love; David's provided a place for shame to hide as his mother used religion to justify child abuse. The psychological foes Romeo was fighting were weakened by his sense of religion; for David they were strengthened by the presence of additional stressors.

Psychological history and change are affected by the unique-ness of the individual's experience. And while some parts of the story are shared, others are not. Over the years as men have told me their stories, I have often been struck by the divergence of paths they have taken to get to the same place—a belief in love. Such journeys necessitate a process of evolving.

THE PROCESS OF EVOLVING INTO LOVE

The Reverend William Gipson, Associate Dean of the Chapel of Princeton University, has summarized some of his views in a brief essay on the essence of love between men and women. Reviewing the path of his own journey, he retraces some steps which other men, perhaps, have also trodden. William is a man whose wisdom I have valued and whose character I deeply respect. He is also my friend. His words appear below.

For me, love links theology and spirituality. The ideas I share here reflect the concrete experiences of love for a heterosexual African American man who is a Christian Minister living out his life in the last decade of the twentieth century.

The Women

There has not ever been a time in my life when women did not love me. My life story is filled with female relatives and friends who have made me feel valued. A proud mother, doting aunts, and a protective sister have provided me with sources of support, care and nurture within the warm bosom of familial embrace. My spouse, former lovers and female friends have each, in distinctive ways, sustained for me a continuous dynamic of love out of which I have learned how to love them back.

The Men

Although women had the central role in my growing-up years, I found it necessary to learn to love men before I had the capacity to love women with maturity and generosity. The men I knew in college—my friends and fraternity brothers—taught me a different kind of intimacy with men than I had ever known. Even today these relationships enrich me. They are treasures.

The Lover

It was my studies in theology which gave me a profound way to understand the experiences of love in my life. Once I was able to accept a model of God as Lover, it seemed that a depthfulness, therefore unknown to me, about love had opened wells of support, care and nurture beyond my wildest imagination. And the wells were within me. I was able to give love with maturity and generosity, because the wells of love do not ever run dry.

The Unfashionable
Spirituality is about making the connection between what is separated, divided, estranged, and the Lover's desire for reconciliation, wholeness and friendship. One's experience of spirituality is a labor of reconciliation.

These endeavors of reconciliation have revolutionary potential. In this regard, they may be viewed as threats by various models and protectors of the status quo. This understanding of love as reconciling power is unacceptable and unfashionable in some social systems. Such resistance to love mirrors its strength. One of my favorite poems, "While Love is Unfashionable" by Alice Walker,[2] captures this idea and has always served as an inspiration for me. It is about fighting for love.

Love is the bridge that allows us to complete the journey back to ourselves and to each other. And while it may be unpopular to speak out in terms of love, it is simply because love is so very powerful.

Commentary

When Reverend Gipson looks back over his journey to becoming a loving man, he sees four stepping stones, each contributing to the meaningfulness of the whole person. He identifies women as providing a wealth of love which he learned to give back to them. Men, particularly those from college years, offered a new experience of intimacy between males. What was shared took place at a closer personal level and such men became lifelong friends. As a theologian, the essence of a loving God became a critical factor for him, carving out a depth of feeling previously unknown within him. And finally, William identifies a loving man as a kind of revolutionary of the heart, similar to that identified by Floyd Thompkins.

Every one of the steps provided him with a unique opportunity for growth. And while each occurred at a different point in his life, the final result was cumulative. The sense of the journey and the traveler become one.

William's perspective is philosophical and theological. He takes steps, ponders them and lets us accompany him. There are also men who, while less pensive or educated, are nonetheless men of love in a world of violence. There are men who work in all professions who have identified as part of their role, a desire to improve unacceptable conditions or help others. Some of these are men in everyday life.

I met a taxi driver in London who rescued lost travelers and a waiter from Central America who was studying international law at night school. Both men try to help others as a way of life; both see their roles as critical; both see themselves as common men.

The taxi driver told me that nine out of ten people who get into his taxi are good people. As a result, he tries to help when trouble arises. Consequently, at times he has found himself in the midst of chaos, surrounded by crowds; has rescued intoxicated individuals from potential muggers to help find their ways safely home; and has maintained a sense of romance with his wife, whom he proposed to on Christmas Eve.

The waiter's family had been displaced by a military takeover. He was studying international law in the hope of helping others whose families had endured similar experiences. Two ordinary men—two missions—two more men of love in a world of violence.

There are many men in everyday life whose stories would fit here. They are the ones who try to add something to the safety and meaning of the daily world through random acts of kindness. I think of the custodian in my elementary school, a heavyset older man who repaired kickballs for the kids and who was followed everywhere he went by a tribe of five young boys who wanted to watch him fix things.

I think of a veterinarian I had once, Dr. Scott, who tried to save a baby goat who was my pet. The vet tried everything, but my goat died of blood poisoning from an infection he had before I got him. I loved that goat and cried and cried when I saw him lying, paralyzed, under the water heater in the laundry room. Dr. Scott couldn't understand why I got so upset over a goat but he respected the intensity and privateness of my feeling. He stayed for nearly two hours—tried everything—but the goat died. He never charged me for his services. Another man of love in a world where unfair and difficult things happen.

Then there is Alex, the young man at a gas station who works two jobs to pay child support and still have enough money to buy the extras he wants for his five-year-old daughter. A veteran, Alex has no training or trade but is a hard worker. In his twenties, he continues to fight the poverty that has tracked his family for generations. To this group add Bill, whose family business was hit by arson. His life's work gone up in smoke, his flower shop ruined and uninsured, he rebuilt it. To lose it was to give up his family's dream.

And then there is Alton, a corrections officer in the local prison who really does care about what happens to the inmates; and Bob, a carpenter who works as a local volunteer fireman, who has saved the lives of several children. I also met Wilson, a retired California police officer who had spent his life waging war against the drug barons of Los Angeles, who had seen several of his police partners gunned down before his very eyes. His satisfaction came from justice. The stories go on and the inner victories are unsung because they are personal. But they are real.

SUMMARY

In spite of the violence they were exposed to, these men not only kept love, they also kept their sense of humanity. Their stories reflect a sense of psychological balance, purpose, and diversity of developmental paths as well as some conceptual similarities.

1. A man's sense of inner safety can provide the base upon which he attempts to make the world a safer place.

2. Emotional risk-taking (whether in terms of reaching across ethnic lines to develop friendships or in bringing harmful

situations into awareness) can have as its source internal personal strength. Referred to by one writer—David Viscott, MD—as *risks of esteem*, such actions require courage.[3]

3. Different philosophical, experiential and cultural bases encourage the development of internal security within men. What is supportive to one might not serve as a support to another.

4. Resources that increase self-efficacy—the sense that "I can do it"—increase the internal strength of the man, who then has a stronger base from which to reach out to others. Security with the self affects the quality of his relationships with others.

5. When no suitable answer to a problem is found, a man of courage may develop his own. This creative approach to problem-solving can contribute to the world. It can make a qualitative difference, whether large or small.

6. The desire to grow and change—to see beyond the way things are and into the way things might be—reflects a personal choice, even if such a choice has its roots in pain.

7. Cynicism is dangerous because it appears to make such good sense. Men who believe in love often accept that the whole picture is somewhere beyond cynicism. And while they might become discouraged and intermittently give up, they continue to work toward that which they believe in. As such, they are not casualties of cynicism.

8. Men of love in a world of violence can serve as positive psychological models for each other. What one man observes from the life of another may provide information which he can use at a later point.

9. There are many ways we evaluate people. We use financial status, educational level, ethnicity, IQ (intelligence quotient) and so on. I think it would be helpful to consider goodness as a personal descriptor. Men of love in a world of violence often have a high GQ—goodness quotient—which can, absolutely, make a difference.

ON A PERSONAL NOTE

Fighting for love in a world of violence often involves seeing the big picture, the whole instead of the parts. Such individuals have the psychological ability to fly up into the atmosphere and look down on the earth from the height of eagles. What they see is not the boundaries between countries or the names of streets, but the whole of the earth. And what they see, they act on.

Having a bigger picture allows one to see from another perspective. Loving mankind or fighting inner battles for self-healing is easier from an overview where lofty thoughts are part of the psychological territory. Practice being an eagle. Everyone can have some of the eagle sight.

PART THREE

Psychological Windows

6 Belief Systems: As a Man Thinketh

Years ago I knew a very angry man. Although Earl was well-known in town and competent in his field, he managed to alienate almost everyone he met. And when he did so, he blamed them for being irrational. Earl believed most people were out to take advantage of him, so he attacked them first. As a result, he pushed away even those who could have been his friends. Earl's belief system—that most people were out to get him—contributed to his anger and spilled over his perceptions like paint, coloring his view of daily events.

I know another man, also eminent in his field. Gilbert, however, has a different belief system and correspondingly different behavior. He accepts that people are essentially good. When he is hurt or disappointed by others he accepts the hurt as an infrequent consequence of his belief system. Consequently, he is inclined to reach out to people, extend himself and maintain relationships of mutual respect. His perceptions allow him to solve problems in a more objective manner than Earl, and when he is wrong, he acknowledges it without blaming others.

Belief systems are the blue prints of the mind. They provide the base upon which the structure of thought rests and directly influence behavior. Building blocks of belief systems involve things like principles, ideas, codes of ethics, and constructs that define our world. These constructs are molded by such social influences as culture, religion, education, family and the person's own individual experience. Belief systems can change with learning.

The examples in this section illustrate how the way men think affects the way they approach situations. Leadership, professional behavior and day-to-day actions all are affected by the content of belief systems.

PROBLEM-SOLVING BEHAVIOR

The Scientific Method

Most scientific discovery occurs through a process known as the scientific method. Scientists attempting to isolate the source of a disease, for example, may identify several viruses and then systematically test each one until they find the virus responsible for the disease. A well-trained scientist is open and objective. Distracters such as superstition and ignorance are sources of error that scientists have been trained to ignore.

Several years ago a colleague of mine, a native of South Africa, was working as a physician in Baragwanath Hospital in Johannesburg. A white, he was treating patients who were members of the Black native population. Dr. Smith was asked to evaluate a patient in the hospital who the predominantly white staff thought was psychotic because he said he heard voices and there was no one there.

Dr. Smith adhered to the scientific method, not the prejudice of the larger community. When the black man, a Bantu from a small village, was brought to him, they discussed the auditory symptoms.

"I hear voices," the patient said, "and no one is there."

"What do the voices say to you?" the doctor asked.

"They say 'Calling Dr. Jones, calling Dr. Smith. Please answer the paging phone.' "

The patient's village was without electrical equipment. He had never heard a loudspeaker before. The man was neither psychotic nor schizophrenic. No one had bothered to ask him what the voices were saying. Given cultural bias, it was easy to see how prejudice could have added a negative interpretation to the man's statements about hearing voices. Adherence to scientific procedure kept the doctor on the trail of the accurate interpretation of the data. Like a contemporary Sherlock Holmes, he based his findings on evidence, not bias. The scientific belief system reduced the error associated with the belief system of prejudice.

There are several types of belief systems that standardize behavior across a variety of situations. Adherence to the scientific method is one example; reliance on ethical principles is another. Behavior guided by such components of a belief system result in consistent outcomes in resolving problems. Perhaps there is no area that depends more on ethical codes than the military as the results can determine matters of life and death.

The next example illustrates a problem-solving approach based on the code of ethics of the United States Air Force Academy.

Ethical Codes

A front-page article of the *New York Times* caught my attention when it appeared on May 1, 1994. Entitled "Air Force Academy Zooms In on Sex Cases," it addressed the recent leadership of Lieutenant General Bradley C. Hosmer in directly approaching problems in sexual harassment at the United States Air Force Academy.[1] The newspaper summary captured General Hosmer's guidance and personal commitment. My telephone interview with him confirmed that his handling of the problem and personal modeling of the Honor Code illustrate the relationship between belief systems and behavior.

A female freshman reported a sexual assault in February 1993. Nine days after the incident, the General—who was concerned about suggestions from additional sources that this might be part of a larger problem on campus—called most of the Academy's female students into the campus auditorium.

He asked for "ground truth" about sexual harassment from the more than 500 female students on campus. For nearly four hours he alone listened to what they had to say. He then met with the male students and asked about their awareness of sexual harassment of female cadets. He listened, then acted.

As a direct result of his leadership, several individuals were asked to leave the Academy; some were disciplined; and investigations resulted in jail sentences for sexual assault perpetrators. In addition, emergency telephone hotlines were set up, and an array of educational programs including human relations training were initiated. At every critical juncture, this basic approach to truth and action was opposite the ineffective handling, for example, of other recently reported cases of sexual harassments of women armed forces members. It was this direct problem-solving approach about which I interviewed him because as a psychologist, I respect it.

My interview with General Hosmer took several directions with a focus on aspects of cognitive psychology. However, his background provides one indication of his depth. A science graduate of the Air Force Academy, former Rhodes Scholar and recipient of a master's degree in international relations from Oxford University, General Hosmer has held a long list of exemplary positions within his military career. Prior to assignment at the Air Force Academy, he was Inspector General in Washington, D.C. He is the recipient of eight major military awards and decorations, including the Distinguished Flying Cross and the Bronze Star Medal with oak leaf cluster. He served in Vietnam and is a command pilot who has flown more than 4,000 hours, principally in fighter aircraft.

Defining the Problem

General Hosmer said,

> For about a year leading up to the event I had been picking up subtle signals that the way we were integrating females into this institution was not as effective as we thought it was.

Through the normal ways of listening, we often get a partial picture. I was alert to considering a nonconventional way of listening. Our goal was to be better at integrating women into our wings. When the sexual assault occurred over Valentine's weekend, I was willing to consider it as the tip of the iceberg, as the assault might only be part of the problem that was brewing. How much it varied from the ground truth was difficult to determine.

However, this was an event that was absolutely unacceptable. We knew we would do something about this but I didn't know what was the right problem to approach. I had data from the previous year (name-calling at the harassment level), but I didn't know where the center of gravity was on this issue. I knew of no other way to find out other than to get the women together. All other options had something negative about them. We needed to do something, and any alternative would have taken too long so that we would have lost the best moment to make a difference.

Creating an Opportunity for Truth

The women cadets were called to a meeting by General Hosmer, who essentially serves as the university president. He could not accurately assess the problem unless they shared with him what they knew. To encourage that sharing, he did several things.

In the auditorium, he dismissed his male aides, removed his insignia of rank and promised the women confidentiality. In addition, he established a note taker, set up boundary conditions and established a flow of dialogue. He told the female cadets what he needed and encouraged them to help him. In his mind, he had a mental picture of how he wanted the meeting to go. He had visualized himself walking around, listening and speaking.

The mental rehearsal was similar to the actual event. The women sensed his sincerity and commitment to action.

Listening

General Hosmer said,

> Part of effective leadership in the military is related to your unit, the entire organization, and not to yourself as an individual. I listened as the female cadets spoke because listening is one of the two or three fundamental skills of command. Leadership assumes team-building, and listening demonstrates interest at a fundamental level. Very often the best solutions to your problems come from the ideas of others.

As he showed, effective listening leads to effective action. The problem was defined as a systems problem, not an individual one affecting only a few women. Information was listened to at the content, emotional and contextual levels, and he acted on it in designing the solution.

Direct Problem Solving

"I need to ask you," I said, "How come you didn't diffuse the issue, refer it to committee, design a questionnaire or otherwise hide from it? Those were organizational alternatives, and have been used effectively by individuals in positions of role power when faced with similar situations. You didn't. Why?"

> They don't work. In 1993 the Lou Harris Poll shared its ratings of public confidence in different careers and occupations. People were asked, "Who do you have trust in?" Fifty-seven percent ranked the military as the highest occupation. Next was ranked the United States Supreme Court Justice with 26 percent. Mutual trust is fundamental to the military profession. It translates into the kind of behavior that takes on a problem straight forward.

Ethics and Honor

I asked him about the relationship between belief systems and behavior, ethics and honor. From a psychological perspective, these are significant issues.

> Honor is personal integrity and again profoundly important to the military profession, which can't function effectively without it. The Air Force Academy has an honor code, and graduates say, "This is what changed my life." Often, the young person first entering has more difficulty adjusting to this than in previous decades, as the larger culture has changed and what's ok is "what my lawyer can do."
>
> Our code is simple: Cadets will not lie, cheat, steal or tolerate those who do. It broadens the role of honor beyond the personal, as is true in a military unit—an organization in which you are totally dependent on the other person's honor. There, you have to insist on the other one's having honor, as someone's life might depend on it.
>
> Honor is part of character. It involves not allowing a convenient misunderstanding to exist.

I had previously explained the premise of this book and its goal related to providing positive life stories and psychological models of men. General Hosmer added:

> I suppose there is almost an intuitive connection between a personality that can be profoundly moved externally with a code like honor and with another external object like a love object. This is only an intuitive sense, but perhaps a connection between honor and love.

From research, I think this would be similar to one's achieving a certain level of moral development. Such a person would have evolved to a level at which the inner resources to adhere to principles and those to emotionally bond both exist.

Leadership

> Leadership is about making the unit effective. I strongly believe in what was written by Sun Tsu, a military writer of 600 BC who said the most effective leader is invisible. All his people know that what they're doing is done well so the unit can continue if he dies. If one is a charger on a white horse, things often collapse under the same situation.

I also asked him about psychological modeling: the idea that each of us can serve as models for other people by providing some new or higher level response to a difficult situation. It is in this area that young people often are discouraged, for they see so few people they want to be like when they grow up.

> Rather than set a model for others to use, I prefer to help others discover what is the right model for them to use for their task. I may not know the answer, but it is foolish for me to say, "This is it." It is often better to help them define their own answer. This approach assumes there's enough time, and it is more permanent.
>
> I operate on the premise that most people will do what they're expected to do; they will act the way they're supposed to act. If the unit is demanding of itself, people will respond. The critical role is what expectations are and how they're communicated. A leader needs to have higher expectations for the self—ones that represent the upper limit.

In summary, this interview illustrates points about the relationship between belief systems and behavior. It also reinforces a premise from the first chapter—that there are men, here a military general who is a university president—who are willing to act on what they know is right and, in doing so, make a difference in the world. Here, that world was the campus life of female cadets.

INTERPERSONAL RELATIONSHIPS

Individual belief systems affect actions towards others, in both professional and personal contexts. One of the beliefs of particular interest here involves parity: being in the same state of power. Equality is a construct fundamental to democracy. Parity is equality applied at a basic, everyday level. The stories in this section illustrate parity as part of a belief system that results in similarities in the behavior of men across different situations. Men who believe in parity listen, respect others and understand that sharing power doesn't mean they get less; it means that the mutual outcome is often more.

Parity

Walter Fox, MD, is a native of Winnipeg, Canada. He has worked in a variety of private as well as public hospitals and outpatient clinics over the course of his forty-five year career. Dr. Fox believes in the concept of parity. As a result, his work with patients has been characterized by mutual learning. We worked together at a clinic some years ago. I was always impressed with his genuine caring for psychiatric patients, who are often treated without dignity by a culture which understands little about mental health. Walter shared some of his ideas in an essay called, *What My Patients Have Taught Me*. It views health care from the other way around—from what providers can learn from those they serve. Parity is implicit here, as one can only learn from those one considers thoughtfully. He recalls a speech by Dr. Karl Menninger in 1944.

It was at the beginning of my career when I first heard him speak. He was presenting on what makes mental hospital care successful. Karl Menninger was a superb teacher, a speaker of flamboyant eloquence and an individual who changed the field of mental health care just by being in it. A giant in the field, his influence affected me as a young psychiatrist. I recall with surprise him speaking about love. He said something like,

> If we can love, this is the touchstone—the key to all therapeutic programs of the contemporary psychiatric hospital. It should dominate the behavior of all staff from the director through the gardener, the housekeeper and clerk. To our patient we can say, "As you and we come to understand you and your life better, the warmth of love will begin to replace anguish, and you will find yourself getting well."[2]

It is significant to note that Walter's comments about Dr. Menninger reflect a dynamic which is still important today: the influence of psychological models and mentors. Something important happens within an individual who comes in contact with another in the same field or walk of life who inspires or offers a new approach to a common situation. The combined effect of ideas and individual can be quite significant. Walter continues:

Now it has never been my habit to talk of love as therapy. I have, however, for a long time realized that genuine caring for a person is sometimes an essential ingredient in a successful therapeutic outcome. It is almost always a significant ingredient in a therapeutic outcome.

When I was thirty-one I was offered a position (which I initially turned down) as superintendent of a state hospital in the southern United States. I was a clinical psychiatrist trained to treat patients and couldn't picture a job taking me away from that and filled with the headaches of administration. A friend of mine who was leaving for a medical mission in Africa encouraged me to take the position, saying, "Knowing *you* and imagining *it*, you will never have another experience like *it* and *it* most likely will never have another experience like *you*." So I took the job and managed to embark on a new unknown journey with the same exciting uncertainty he felt. It was at that state hospital that I started learning from my patients.

This is the third professional man in this chapter to be characterized as open-minded. The others—Dr. Smith and General

Hosmer—along with Dr. Fox have maintained a belief system that includes assumptions to insure this at a basic level. Dr. Fox continues explaining what he learned.

Learning to Question Rules

As part of my role as chief hospital administrator, I made it my responsibility to visit psychiatric patients in a variety of work and therapeutic settings within the hospital. This is how I met Mary.

It was in the hospital kitchen area I first noticed Mary. In her early forties, she was running an initial phase of our dietary department's food production (usually vegetable preparation and cooking). While active in doing this she also supervised a number of patient helpers with gentle reminders, clear directions and cheerful encouragement. She had to be a patient, I told myself, as she was not in uniform, but what was she doing in a mental hospital?

I went over, introduced myself, and after a brief encounter decided to find out why she was numbered among the state hospital's some 2,500 patients.

It was Walter's interest in Mary as a person as well as his clinical background as a doctor that made him pursue this line of inquiry. Caring, clinical observation, curiosity and concern motivated him to follow up on his meeting with this woman. To many administrators, contact with such a patient would simply have been written off as unimportant. However, when parity is involved, what happens to one person is important. Dr. Fox resumes his story:

Mary was forty-two years old and had been committed to the hospital in 1944, some twelve years previously, for what is now called schizophreniform disorder. She had been married to a local man who had served in World War II and perhaps because of that was away a lot in the initial months of her hospitalization. At least there were no records of any visitation. Chart records revealed an attempt to reach the spouse had been unsuccessful, and there was a note that he had moved to the northeast, address unknown.

In those days, commitment to a state hospital carried with it legal determination of incompetency. Mary was legally incompetent; she could not leave the hospital without a next of kin to sign her out. This latter requirement was not actually in the law but had been established practice for as long as the hospital could remember. As I thumbed through the yellowed pages of her file, the wording of the commitment papers began to take on new meaning. "And she, in this case Mary S., shall be committed to the care of the superintendent until such time as she has been determined to have been restored to competence."

Legally and clinically, Mary was under my care. So, we talked about what to do. Her parents were dead, she had no friends or relatives in the area, and yes, she would love to get out of the hospital. We decided on a strategy.

Realizing that there were options within his control, Dr. Fox decided to act on what he saw as best for the patient. He and she discussed the situation and came up with an action plan. The problems would be approached directly, even if in a way somewhat unusual in terms of the institution's history. He used the role power of his office to help her achieve a better life after asking her what she wanted for herself. It was teamwork at a fundamental level.

We decided Mary would read the classified ads, get outfitted in clothes appropriate for job hunting from the donated clothing room, get a little money for several fifty-cent bus fares into the center of town and get a job. Then, she would live at the hospital until she saved enough to pay for room and board.

Mary did well and soon was living independently on her own. What did I learn from her? She taught me to question established institutional practice enough, in her case, to even disregard it. She also taught me to be on the outlook for patients who spoke and even more importantly behaved productively and question their need for continued institutionalization. Often such people, in making a functional contribution to the institution, can appropriately make the transition to the community. All of this I learned, and Mary began my education.

Learning to Listen

Walter continues, "Next I would like to share what I learned from patients when I listened to them rather than lectured them."

In terms of power, it is important to understand the difference between lecturing and listening. Lecturing to another person is done from a superior relationship position. In other words, the one with more power (the lecturer) tells something to the one with less power (the listener). The communication tends to be one way—a sender and a receiver. On the other hand, listening involves a position of more equal power: one person (the speaker) shares something with another person (the listener) who then understands the first person better. The listener is free to ask questions or gather more information in a way that someone in an audience seldom feels free to do.

When I was state hospital superintendant, one of the behaviors that bothered me most was patients sorting through our sixty-gallon trash cans that dotted the hospital grounds. Behaviors like this typically resulted in my giving a lecture which went something like this: "Joe, your job and mine is to achieve your discharge from the hospital. You must develop skills and behaviors consistent with living in the real world."

One summer day I approached a rather elderly man who was digging through a sixty-gallon garbage can. The rote lecture on my tongue was ready to spring out, but from somewhere inside came a sense that sometimes guides me against my most pious and heartfelt wrong intentions. I found myself somehow saying, "Good morning, Mr. Thomas. Now just what are you digging around in there for?"

Behavior is goal-directed. A belief in parity inclines one to explore the reason for the behavior and withhold the lecture. So Walter followed his belief system and initiated a conversation with the patient.

> Mr. Thomas: "Oh, hi, Doc. I'm looking for a piece of cardboard, 15×15 or larger. I can always cut it down to size."
> Me: "And what do you need that for?"
> Mr. Thomas: "Well, you see Doc, ever since you put that floodlight in the back parking lot, well, I know it was necessary with all that pilfering that was going on, but that light shines right through the windowpane into my eyes. You know, I like to look out my window at the stars and moon and the trees before I go off to sleep. So I figure if I can block out the direct beam through that one pane, maybe I can have that pleasure again."
> Please note: my patient had asked for nothing but told me what I didn't know.

Again, this is a comment on parity. We learn from information shared in the context of viewing a person as worthy of respect, a type of affiliative power.

Dr. Fox continues:

> We then went to the patient's bed on his unit. I lay in his bed with my face to the window and sure enough, through that 15×15 pane of glass, there was the bright business end of the offending floodlight, even at mid-day. I could imagine how irritating that thing would have been after dark.
>
> It was a simple matter to modify the shield on the floodlight so that it shone on the vehicles it was supposed to protect and not into the eyes of Joe Thomas or his friends sleeping in that building. By listening to him speak (instead of myself lecture), we were able to make our institution a somewhat more desirable place (if one must live in an institution). Joe and many others taught me how much we can learn to make a place more liveable if we only listen to those who live there.

There is much more to be shared than can be presented here.

The patient stories Dr. Fox used to illustrate the concept of shared power in professional relationships—here, between doctor and patient—provide a contrast to the hierarchical models in which the doctor, from a position of superiority, is always right. Such actions involve a set of beliefs about the nature of relationships and the allocation of power within those relationships.

Identity in Men Involved with Women of Power

This section involves the stories of three men involved with powerful women. Two are married to business executives; one shares what he learned from his experience with a woman who subsequently became a Ph.D. clinical psychologist. All three men see their identity as a man as separate from the relationship and enhanced by the status of the woman they are involved with. In their belief system, association with a wife's or girlfriend's status does not diminish or detract from their identity as a man; it is viewed as a plus. It enriches the relationship.

Larry is a thirty-four year old American whose father's grandparents were born in Italy and his mother's in Poland. He is single, an industrial engineer and a man who has worked hard since age fourteen when he got his first job. His friends are both single and married, in their twenties and thirties. An attractive man who lifts weights, works out and owns an Arabian horse, Larry shared some of his beliefs about himself as a man involved with a professional woman (a Ph.D. clinical psychologist).

If men in the eighties were into money, men in the nineties are into love. I think it involves intimacy, a sharing type of love with sex as one part. Both people give to the relationship. It's not all the man's responsibility. Each person can survive on their own—it's not that they can't live without each other or that the other person is somehow attached so they're living through you. Each has self-respect as well as respect for the partner. You have respect for the other person's opinion and don't expect them always to agree with you.

I have some friends who can't accept their wife not agreeing with them. They take it as criticism when it's just that she has a different view because she's a different person. After being with my partner so long, I respect that she's very smart and has a way of looking at things that's different from mine. And she can tell me in a manner that doesn't hurt or offend me. That I can accept this without viewing it as a negative says I have self-esteem.

One part of the belief system, here, involves the acceptance of differences and another part involves the presence of self-esteem. Another involves a positive self-image—the man sees himself as a valuable, whole person and the relationship with the woman as a place for mutuality of exchange.

When a man sees himself with a professional woman, he's still the same person—he doesn't have to view himself any differently; it's just she's open to different opinions and ideas from the guy because she can stand her ground just like I can stand my ground. If a woman is not professional, she might think she shouldn't stand up to you and just go by your opinion because you're the man or the one with more self-esteem and confidence. When a woman does stand up for her opinion, I see her as having a lot of self-confidence and self-esteem.

Some of Joan's opinions have opened my eyes to a different perspective. After being with her I could never go back to a woman who had no professional ambition, no opinions or low self-esteem. I've come to learn that I really value her judgment, and we respect each other. And we have learned so much from each other.

Reciprocity is maintained—the give and take of a relationship—and also applies to the mutuality of sharing information. Here, Larry explains that it adds a dimension of interest in a relationship he is not willing to do without.

He also adds this:

My parents didn't have a relationship like this—neither had been to college and my mother was a traditional person. She raised the kids, and my father brought home the income. I learned an alternate model from my first girlfriend—at fifteen—and it continued to develop over time.

Within this context, differences enhance the relationship; they don't detract from it.

She was smarter than I was, but we just grew a lot together and were able to share. There were analytical things in her life that I liked, and things that were not so analytical in my life that she liked. It was never a difference of who was better. We never gave each other that feeling. Even though I envied her intelligence as she is very smart, I was recreational and more skilled in some ways that was just a good mix. She encouraged me to put more emphasis on my education, and I encouraged her to be more fun-loving. Each person was equal but in different realms.

The benefits? Larry goes on to explain that he wouldn't want a traditional relationship in which the woman is at his beck and call. Instead, he identifies the gains in one type of power (affiliative) exchanged for another (coercive or "beck and call" power).

For me, a good relationship is one that gives me the chance to grow independently without feeling the weight of the world on my shoulders. Things become not my sole responsibility or obligation (like the children or the house) but our decision (it's ours, not mine. It brings self-worth to both of us, not just one.) And I like that.

The stories of two other men echo some of the same ideas. They have, in their belief systems, elements that make it possible for them to maintain successful behavior toward themselves and the women they are married to. In both cases, they describe the women, who work in very different fields than they do, with respect and appreciation. One man, Derek, was born in Ireland; the other one, Robert, is Italian-American.

Derek Petersen, 30, describes the transition from being single to being married, which he went through a few years ago. He married an advertising executive highly regarded in her field.

When you're single, you make your own decisions. When you're in a relationship, you have to accept the other's influence. I think this is harder for the man to accept—the woman's influence. When I was single, I thought the man was always right. However, I married an advertising executive—and now I find myself standing back to think about what she said. I find myself often realizing that she has a point. This was a change for me. I was raised with the idea that the man did all the thinking.

I was born in Dublin and in my background, the father was the one in control of everything. My mother had influence over the meal and the home. My father, who was a taxi driver all his life, had control of the rest. When he passed away, I had to go out and sort everything out because I was the son.

In my marriage we're both doing the work. My wife will ask me to do something and I'll do it. I'm easygoing and she tends to worry. There's a balance because we're so different, although it's hard sometimes, too.

Again, here part of the belief system is that different does not mean bad—it's just different—and can be a source of balance in a relationship. Also, in an open and objective belief system, a man's identity comes fundamentally from a belief in himself. Therefore, the focus is on him and not a set of fixed behaviors. In Ireland and in his family growing up, the male did the thinking and had the control. However, in Derek's present home, both partners share the thinking as well as the work to be done. In addition, emotional commitment is strong.

I'm more willing to listen than I have been in other relationships. This is for fifty years, not until the next one comes along. I only want one marriage and this is it. What is it about this one that makes me feel that way? I enjoy being with her and I never get bored. We don't have a lot of the same hobbies but we can talk. She's a good person, she's strong, and she is good for me as well. She's very organized and together. And physical appearance is part of it.

Part of his transition, then, was brought about by a desire to be with this particular woman. The motivation for change came from a sense of the comfort and enjoyment he felt with Marie and the knowledge that this was not the type of woman who wanted to have him do the thinking for her. Derek continued:

I had a tendency of holding back—I know that's a male thing. I'd let something build up and then be mad—in a bad humor—and then I'd let it out and give Marie a hard time instead of confronting the problem here and now. She has more of a tendency if she has a problem to deal with it straight away.

And a reference to parity again:

In other relationships I was always in control. This one—she has just as much input and I had to get used to that. This one wasn't so easy. With other women I pretty much went out when I pleased. With this one I had to get used to not always being in charge and let her have more. Subconsciously, I think I want to control her, but I'm also fairly proud of her and what she can achieve. I'm happy she has a great job, makes a good income and is an interesting person. I really love Marie, want to spend time with her and have always been quite thankful for the good things that have come my way.

Derek has included the importance of achieving goals into his belief system. And that she is a person of achievement is something he values about Marie as well.

I work hard and have been appreciative of my good luck. And I keep doing things—making long-term plans, achieving in school and building a business. I can't just bob along; I have to be aiming for things.

Larry, Derek, and other men who value women of achievement, then, have a sense of achieving of their own. Their belief systems about being a man and being with a woman of high status are congruent; that is, they see no problem with having both together.

One final vignette in this section is shared by Robert Leone, an Italian-American who works as a hair stylist at a local salon. Fundamentally an artist, Robert is successful in his field and has a loyal clientele among wealthy Princeton families. His wife Georgia is a business executive who flies around in the corporate jet and is picked up by the company limousine when her plane lands.

The two met years ago when they both had an interest in cosmetology. He owned and operated two salons; she had just graduated from a training program. They attended a business seminar at a local hotel, and Robert and a colleague, both attendees, were just leaving the dining room. As he walked out into the hotel lobby, Robert saw a young woman seated in a large woven wing-back chair. The chair was so large and the woman so small that the contrast was surprising. When he glanced over, their eyes met—just for an instant—and then he was gone.

Later that morning, as the seminar was about to begin, the same woman entered the classroom and sat down beside Robert. They started talking and were together the rest of the weekend. Their first date was spent at a friend's wedding; the second was with other friends for a week in Florida; and then they became engaged. They were married approximately seven months later and have been together ever since.

In the mind of her husband, she is still the same small young woman he saw sitting in that big, big chair in 1973, more than twenty years ago. They are both artistic; relate on the level of beauty as well as shared values about love, family, cooking and opera; and are still happy with themselves and each other.

The paradigm here involves a visual picture of the essence of the person—in this case, the wife—which remains unchanged though the status of the woman has changed in the outside world. In the husband's belief system, the wife's success is one element of her person; the original image is the essence and so he remains unthreatened. He is pleased with her success and shares the happiness with her. He is her biggest fan.

SUMMARY

This chapter presents one idea in many contexts. The importance of a belief system is reviewed here, along with its relationship to behavior.

1. Men's belief systems affect their behavior.

2. Some belief systems are healthier than others. As a result, some men's behavior is healthier than others.

3. There are certain kinds of belief systems—application of the scientific method, reliance on codes of ethics, belief in parity, for example—which result in similar functioning across situations. The men might be different but their actions may be comparable.

4. Men whose belief system includes sharing power listen. By sharing power and listening, problems are more readily solved and new directions are attainable.

5. Men who become involved with women of accomplishment may do so because they choose to and because they find doing so congruent with maintaining a personal identity as a loving, valuable man.

ON A PERSONAL NOTE

Belief systems are acted out in behavior. As they change, so does behavior. This principle is perhaps the most important reason for choosing a continuing commitment to personal growth and change. Learning is a lifelong process; it does not stop with high school or college graduation. It does not stop with union acceptance or professional status attainment. It goes on.

The world is constantly changing. Science and technology are evolving. Definitions of formalized religion, spirituality, economic security, nationalism and even love are being restructured. The ability to learn and grow allows us to keep equilibrium. Understanding allows us to recognize what is out-of-balance and make adjustments. It is part of being self-aware.

For Mick

Once in awhile
  someone comes along
who is
  what you believe in
and who,
by actions,
confirms for you
that those beliefs are real.
A hero
yet someone very human.

You are for me that person.
Time has passed
since first we met—
and longer still
since we shared time—
but the way you are
and the way I see you
remains unchanged.
I see you now
as I saw you then
  kind
  loving
of courage.

I love you for your goodness.[1]

7 Behavior: Integrity's Mirror

His voice is filled with both pride and humility. He is a sixty-five year old retired police officer from Wisconsin named Harry Jansen, but he is best known as the father of the United States Olympic speed skater, gold medalist Dan Jansen. Harry said,

> When I was growing up, what it meant to be a man was that you would raise a family, be a good provider and be there when you were needed. That's the way my dad was, a friend and advisor. He tried to show love just by being available when you needed him, and I think that was my idea, too.
>
> Let me give you an example. I'm afraid of heights but I bought a two-story house which needed painting. I was up on a ladder, scared to death, trying to paint. My dad came over—he was sixty-five at the time—and said, "You can't do that if you're afraid of heights." So he got up on the ladder and painted the top windows, and I painted the lower ones. It's kind of embarrassing, but he was there for me.
>
> And in my role as a father, I tried to do this, too. When Dan was skating I was the business manager for the skating team. In the three years I was business manager, I think the time I was the most helpful was in 1992 when he was the world record holder. It was in France at the Olympic Games, and he got fourth place. We both sat in the dressing room, kind of in shock—he was expected to win, and he expected to win. In all the World Cup meets that year he had placed first or second. The only question was whether he would get

the gold or silver medal. Instead, there was no medal; only huge disappointment for him.

Anyhow, we were sitting there, in the quiet for what seemed like a long time. Finally I said, "You are still my hero. You gave it your best shot. We'll get through this—it isn't the end of the world—we've gotten through worse things than this." We hugged and both said "I love you," and we both felt better.

Mr. Jansen's statements reflect that love is about actions. His father was there to help him paint—not just watch him. He was there with his son to face defeat—not just observe him. What a man does speaks louder than what he says. And behavior that is consistent over time creates trust.

How a man responds to a situation is linked to what he thinks and feels as well as how he defines himself. The stories in this chapter capture how men show their caring by the way they behave—through the language of actions. The common theme is that they choose what they believe in and maintain their integrity in doing so.

Being There

Mr. Jansen continued,

I wanted to be there for any troubles or problems that arose with the kids. And yet I wanted them to learn to make their own way. These ideas were pretty well set, I guess, while I was young because I learned them from my dad. My mother died when I was fifteen, and he didn't have to say he loved us because we knew. He was there for us. I tried to be the same way, but I felt freer to say I loved my children, because society was changing and access to television and the media showed men more freedom in showing affection to their children. They got married, were grown, but I continued to tell them anyway and they do value it.

In the years that Dan worked towards his goal, I knew he was the best skater in the world at that time. The Olympics are just one race—although it was hard to remember that when we were sitting there in that locker room in France. He had had tremendous difficulties to overcome; he skated in the 1988 Olympics the day his sister died. He fell. And he fell a week later, too. It's a wonder he could go out on the ice at all. But he did it for himself, for his family and his sister. He always kept trying.

I loved him and always believed in him. Dan is exceptional and always has been to me. He was the world sprint skating champion in 1988 and 1994 and has broken eight world records. Presently he holds the world record in the 500 meter race and was winner of the gold medal in speed skating in the 1000 meters in the 1994 Olympics in Norway. He never gave up and love was always there beside him.

How does being there show what I value? My wife Gerry and I feel the same way. You want to be there when they need you because your family is the most important thing in the world.

Being available, being present in the life of someone a man loves is a choice based on personal values. It is the behavioral component of emotional bonding. Men show love in many different ways, and loving behavior is part of emotional process. As Mr. Jansen observes, times have changed, and men are freer to share thoughts and feelings. Television and the media reflect some of that change as well as promote it. Contemporary men are more free to act on the still small voice of the heart. They listen more intently and often choose to make it a leading force in their lives. In overcoming obstacles along the way their actions mirror integrity.

Mr. Jansen felt a deep belief in his son that made a difference. With such support, Dan Jansen's life was changed. The result of such teamwork was an Olympic gold medal. The long-term result is a loving family unit. Few things can match the positive power of such an influence. It is the behavioral manifestation of love.

More modern men are choosing to *be there*, to be more available for their children and the women they love. And they use that word—choosing. It is a conscious act motivated by a way they want to see themselves and how they define loving.

Per Bjarte Hanstveit, the head of director staff of a Norwegian electricity company, has similar feelings, which are reflected in his actions. At thirty-nine, Per Bjarte reports that he has changed a lot since he first received his master of science degree in electricity at the age of twenty-five.

I made a very fast career. After five years I was at the top level reporting to the company CEO who was my boss. I was advancing professionally at an accelerated pace and spent very much time on work, not so much with my family. Then I made a major change—I altered my priorities.

With thoughtfulness, he continued:

I think the biggest change for men comes when children are born. It used to be that when a child was born, the father would hold it when it was fully prepared—after the birth, cleaned, and in dry diapers. Now, even participation in the birth of the baby is a requirement of society, and the children themselves learn in school that you should do things with them, not just for them. Fathers are involved in cleaning, washing the baby, waking up at midnight to care for the sick child, and so on. In Norway both parents work, and it used to be that just the mother would get up with the child who was ill. Now fathers do, too; both parents participate actively in the raising of the kids. You follow up with the school and the same with all sports. The requirement is that you do things with your child: play with them, help them with their home lessons. It is a requirement of time. You should be in the center of it, not just standing outside telling them what to do or not to do.

Being there, this Norwegian father feels, is a requirement. And he has made different choices in his life because of it.

Before I had children I thought my career was the most important thing. I worked hard to get ahead and was living in Bergen. My wife Sylvi Ann and I had a long talk and decided we wanted a different kind of lifestyle for our children. So I changed jobs, and we moved back to the small island where we grew up. It is a much slower pace there, and the network of our family support is there. In Fotlandsvaag where we grew up—my grandfather knew her grandfather—we have a much extended family, and it is good for our children. My wife helped me see the importance of influences on the children, and we made value of life our priority.

A few years ago I would have said my most important role as a man was to earn money, but now I say it is to raise my family and give my children a good future. Children change your point of view. You want to give them the best basis for their lives.

My wife and I show each other much affection—and this is different from our Norwegian culture, which I think can seem emotionally cold because people are not so expressive with their feelings. We try to help our children to express feelings—both happiness and sorrows—and we try not to hide our feelings. Sylvi Ann and I kiss, hold hands, and hug in front of the children. We want them to see this is part of life and that people who love each other take care of each other.

For a man, being there involves making different choices, following through on behavior he thinks is right, and evaluating his priorities. While all of this is happening, he takes stock of himself and his life. As time goes on, the accounting system he uses sometimes changes.

I have always loved my wife's independent qualities, but as time goes on and as I come to see the work she does with the children, I come to respect her more. If I had the idea that rich was only money, then because I earn more money, I would be the most valuable person in the family. But because I value other things than money—the children and the family—then I don't think I'm the most important. You can't count money or measure the value of what is most important in life with money or moneymaking.

Remember the comments in Chapter 6 on belief systems and their effect on behavior? Without having read that chapter, Per Bjarte gives a crystal summary.

> When you are young you want to be rich and have a nice car. When I grew up, we didn't have much money, and so of course I wanted to be rich. But when you grow older the meaning of the word *rich* changes. It is not money but the value of life that makes one rich.

As a man evolves, his concept of *rich* changes, and so do his actions related to increasing and protecting his wealth. The standard measure changes from money-based units to those involving intangibles such as hugs, laughter and love. Dimensions determining worth vary with understanding; some wealth is able to be calculated and some is beyond measure.

When concepts change, behavior may follow. However, the reverse is true also. Sometimes, the act of successfully handling difficult situations teaches a man that what appears impossible simply is something that takes a little longer to figure out.

Persistence

"Refusing to relent; continuing, especially in the face of opposition" is how *Webster's New World Dictionary* defines persistence.[2] How is this related to men who believe in love? The next story is a modern version of an old classic—William Shakespeare's *Romeo and Juliet*—with a different ending. And the variable was one man's tenacious refusal to let go of love.

In the classic love story, the lives of two young lovers are lost when they are forbidden to marry. The families are feuding and the lovers "star-crossed'; the outcome is foreshadowed from the Prologue:

> *Two households, both alike in dignity,*
> *In fair Verona, where we lay our scene,*
> *From ancient grudge break to new mutiny,*

Where civil blood makes civil hands unclean.
From forth the fatal loins of these two foes
A pair of star-crossed lovers take their life,
Whose misadventured piteous overthrows
Doth with their death bury their parents'strife.[3]

Our young lovers are born not in Verona but in India.

Their families are alike in social class but from different
communities.
It is not ancient grudge but ancient tradition which causes
the strife
as from the families of two different groups these two are
born
and therefore cannot marry.
Their difficulty arouses pity but is,
with persistence and creativity, resolved.

The story is being told by Vineet, a physician in his mid-
thirties who, like the Shakespearean character Romeo, was
required to give up the woman he loved. He, however, had
other ideas.

In India we have different castes in the Hindu religion, and
there are something like 200 to 300 separate sects in the
Hindu religion. It means that the foods we eat, the languages
we speak at home and the idols we use for worship are not
the same. Sometimes there are also differences about how
money, character, and even behavior are perceived. From the
parents' point of view (and that of the culture), people should
get married within the same community so there is little
difference. We are both from the upper classes within our
own communities, but the geography there gives you an
identity. Where you are from largely determines how you do
things, and parents often want to keep their children from
marrying outside their own sect to protect them from potential problems that might develop because of differences.
These ideas are strongly rooted in the culture and historically
have exerted much influence over the lives of young people.

My older sister fell in love with a young man from a different region. There was much opposition to that, and so she relented and eventually married someone from the same community. And the resistance was on both sides—our family and his. The man's parents persuaded him, and my parents did the same to my sister. She was very upset about it for a long time. Eventually she got over it and married someone else, but it was very hard for her. I saw what happened so I never brought it up with my parents. I knew how strong their belief was.

The stage is now set—not for a feud or familial grudge, but for conflict. Two people from different communities cannot marry. Period. Enter Reema. Vineet continues,

We met in the eleventh year at school and were part of a large group of friends, as are most students in India. We'd meet on weekends; we called each other and would talk about our experiences. We both wanted to be physicians and had similar hopes and dreams. Anyhow, group activities are a very common form of socializing. And then the twelfth year came, a very big one—very busy—and filled with many picnics, meetings and get-togethers at other people's houses. Reema and I saw each other a lot. Often, I would organize the group events so I might see her more.

It was during the next year—the thirteenth year—that I realized I started wanting to meet and keep in touch. Around the fourteenth year I had told one of my friends I was sure I was in love with her, but I knew my elder sister had had a similar experience. She was not able to get my family's support and I would not be either.

We didn't speak about how we felt about each other until the fifteenth and sixteenth year. Reema eventually came to me and said, "I want to talk about us."

The conflict is set. Two young people are in love and cannot be together because of cultural tradition that is not open to negotiation. Here, the young man must choose between two loves: family and Reema. With either choice, he loses something of extreme value to him. In the Shakespearean tragedy, death results. Here a different path is taken.

I wanted both my family and Reema. I was dependent on my parents and told Reema, "This is how I feel about you. I'm ok about any kind of agreement, but the future is uncertain until I become independent from my parents."
She thought about this for two or three months and she decided she also loved me. We decided to be together and thought of a plan.

Enter a problem-solving model. Romeo and Juliet declare their love and make a decision to devise a third alternative—one that allows them to keep their families and each other. The plan also allows them to pursue their dreams.

We both wanted to be physicians, and the best medical schools are in the United States. So we decided to go to America for future studies. However, we knew that if we talked to our parents about our love for each other, that her parents would approach mine and there would be a big problem.
So we applied for further education and both of us got admission. We went to separate universities—I went to Harvard, she to Stanford—and then a year later I transferred. I had gotten some financial assistance, which made it easier for me. Before that, we had a lot of expensive phone bills.

The plan includes education—which both people want—and travel outside the country. However, parental acceptance is still an obstacle. There is more to be resolved.

My parents had known her from her exposure with this large group of friends, and her parents knew me pretty well. When I transferred to Stanford, I told my parents that the professional opportunities would be better and that Reema would help me become acclimated to campus. Her parents accepted that two friends would be at the same exceptional university. My parents said, "He wouldn't even think about being serious with her." After that they gave the matter little additional attention.

Finally, we were nearly through school, and in order for us to get married, she needed to get her parents' permission. So I wrote my family also. I was nearly supporting myself with a research grant and was independent. We wanted them to know what the situation was—that this would be something in the future. Reema's parents replied positively; mine were very upset and made me promise to break off the relationship. I said I would.

The couple had presented to the parents a logical case, a united front. They had made known their intentions for the future, although nothing had happened yet. Parental approval was important both culturally and personally. Vineet and Reema loved their own families, and each valued the family of the other. By design, no one was supposed to get hurt. However, the cultural rules had been set and there was little room for compromise.

For the next year no one discussed the issue with Vineet's parents. It was assumed that the problem had been resolved. It was getting closer to graduation, and Vineet wanted to again approach his parents. He went back to India to visit them with the idea of discussing it with them. He and Reema had decided that if they didn't agree, the couple would marry in the United States. Vineet continues:

When I went back, I was told that my mother wasn't well. She had developed an inoperable brain tumor, and I was told she had a year to live. Obviously, I did not bring up the topic of marriage.

I returned to the United States, made my professional plans, and we got married through the court. We called her parents, who were happy for us. I had been offered a good position and attended a world health conference that allowed me to visit India again. This time I was told my mother had only a few months to live. I wanted her to know Reema and I had married, but the medical staff told me it was not advisable.

Sometimes, when all else fails, someone reaches out to help and, in that against-the-odds effort, is successful. Enter the sister.

> I had explained the situation to my elder sister, and she decided she would help. She spoke to my father and also my mother on my behalf. She convinced them that it would be a good thing to let me get married in India while mother was still there to be part of it. This time the family agreed. Reema had been at the same world health conference and so she was there, too. We made the necessary arrangements and had a small marriage in the traditional way in India.
>
> Not long after that my mother died. My father accepted Reema, who had been able to spend some time with mother during those last days. He had seen how kind she had been and the respect she had always shown for my parents. In addition, my parents had always liked her. All of this happened nearly ten years ago, and things have continued to go well for us within the family.

There are several critical elements to Vineet's story. First, he took his own feelings seriously. When he realized the depth of emotion he and Reema shared, he acted on that in a consistent manner. Instead of leaving or giving up, he was committed to his emotions. Second, he decided to approach the situation in a logical way.

> I took a problem-solving approach. I did this because I didn't want to upset my parents, and, at the same time, I didn't want to sacrifice my love for her. I had to find a way and I knew I could.

And Vineet didn't give up. He persisted.

> At one point I lost hope, but I went ahead and decided that I didn't want to lose this love. What happened was that they changed and accepted her.

Finally, he acted on what he knew he needed to do.

> The decision to get married was a crucial one. And I was

lucky that my mother accepted Reema. It made it easier for my father.

When men believe in love, they don't give up. They persist in looking for a way to bring about a positive outcome, for they realize love is special.

Changing

Fear accompanies change, which often ushers in the unknown. The men who tell their stories in this section have looked into the face of change and, looking back, would do so again. While their stories are as different as the men who tell them, you will a notice a common theme.

Shawn

My father is without honor, and the nature of his behavior is beyond what can be shared here. He is a well-known person in his profession, and as a result, wields much power. We have not spoken in ten years—from the time I understood just what it was that he did. He is a miserable human being.

The speaker, thirty-five, is an earnest man with intense eyes. He described his process of change in terms of his own developing sense of identity.

From an early age I had a sense of what it was to be a man. It meant that one was the breadwinner, a worker, and that men traveled a lot and spent time away from their families. I learned early that men were definitely very dominant. They were the kings of their castles.

Does Shawn see himself that way?

Well, all of those things applied to me until ten years ago—and then I started thinking of myself as an individual, not part of a group or stereotype. I felt that to be classified as a man I had all those definitions to live up to—a lot of pressure. And then I realized the macho stuff was just BS. I just stopped worrying about how other people would view my masculinity or my machismo—because it all stopped when I stopped talking to my father. All that time the main person I was trying to impress was him, and he was someone not even worthy of my respect. After that I started being myself and seeing myself instead of trying to live up to expectations. It feels a lot better.

Shawn's father had physically attacked Shawn's mother and younger sister, and it was Shawn who called the police. They have not spoken since.

It took a little while to become my own man. The funny thing is that all the time I was expecting to become my own man—like being knighted—by pleasing my father and making him proud of me. When I broke my relationship with him, I realized he had nothing to do with it. Once I was happy with who I was there was no need for a medal. There weren't really that many things I needed to change in myself, and all this time, he had been telling me how unacceptable I was.

I think what made the difference was that I started placing a high priority on feelings—myself and those of others. And that occurred as I started changing. You have to pay a lot of attention to your feelings—don't ignore them; don't distort them—that's the most important thing. If you don't understand your feelings, you can't take another step forward. There are so many things you can't do if you're not in touch with your feelings. Good feelings are good, and bad feelings are good, too. They can tell you things you need to know.

My father was involved in some things I didn't think were right. He made it seem like I was stupid or uncool—how come I didn't get it? That's not what was going on. He was the Black Knight and I was the White Knight. We were at odds but not because of me—because some of the things he did were not right.

Sometimes young people are on higher levels of moral development than the people who are supposed to be teaching them right from wrong. Although this situation is not that frequent, when it does occur, it creates difficulty in the mind of the child and takes a while to sort out. Confusion and fear can eat away at the fabric of self-worth. The young man wanders in and out of self-doubt.

For years I was afraid that I couldn't be a father—that I couldn't love children and be good with them because I never had any decent role models as far as parenting is concerned. My father never lived with me, and my stepfather was not very emotional. I thought, how could I be a good father when I've never had one? But now I know differently. I have watched my father-in-law with his kids and my three brothers-in-law with their children, and I've learned a lot. Being a good father is something you choose. It's a way you choose to act. I love my children with tenderness because I remember what it was to be young, and now I know that the shadow of the missing loving father from the past does not determine my life. I do.

How does he explain the changing process?

What I had to do was give up the past in order to gain the future.

Some men are faced with situations like this one. They have to choose the kind of life they want for themselves and the kind of man they want to be. As in Shawn's case, the options are not always obvious, and the memories associated with an absent, mean or sociopathic father often require some psychological housecleaning. Men like Shawn are trying to free themselves from the "like father, like son" dictum which haunts their inner core and steals their dreams. When they are successful, they achieve a victory that promotes a different type of lifestyle than they had as a child and a different type of love relationship than their parents shared.

The psychological modeling process is a powerful one. However, research has concentrated on modeling cruel individuals as opposed to loving ones. The model of cruelty results in a chain of aggression through a process of identification with the aggressor. (Person A slaps Person B who then slaps Person C, and so on.) Identification with one who is loving can result in breaking the chains of the past.

A man with a cruel father, having observed more compassionate men, may choose to emulate the healthy model. The stories of David, Phil, and Shawn illustrate such a choice. For men like them, positive role models were found in a variety of places. They were a grandfather, a man who lived in the neighborhood, and a father-in-law. Exposure to positive models can be powerful because such men provide behaviors with a better fit for love. As the culture changes and more positive models are available to men, the shadow of a hurtful parent is lifted by choosing love.

Jim Anderson

Jim Anderson is an Australian farmer who raises grains such as wheat and barley as well as sheep for wool production. Educated at home and abroad, he comments on the cultural mirror for men.

We have a tradition not unlike America, to show a degree of respect and kindness but not to do it in the manner of a Casanova. If one shows too much emotion—love or warmth—it is seen as somewhat effeminate. Traditionally, Australians have an image of ourselves, which is not especially true, as an image of a fun-loving, manly nation with the strong, silent-type man. In years gone by Australia was thought to be a man's country. Men did a lot of things without their wives.

Here is one way the culture mirrors the change for men. The stereotype of our folklore in farming is represented by our seasonal workers, the shearers, men who shear sheep. They would be physically strong, chauvinistic, hard-driving, hard-swearing. That is the role they occupied in the past, although there are more women now who work in the shearing industry.

Recently at a shearing we had these men in our shed. In the past they would have talked about booze, women, sport. This time their conversation during meal breaks centered on their young kids. I was just amazed how much things have changed. In years gone by if a woman walked by a shearing shed, a call went out "ducks on the pond," which meant the men had to behave themselves—swearing and rough language had to stop. Now there could be women in the shed working and the shearers' language is toned down a great deal. The shearers on a small scale are reflective of change on a large scale. Men don't see it as being effeminate or weak or strange to show warmth, concern, and love. Where did the change come from? It evolved with the society. But why does the society evolve? I don't know.

Change, then, can be viewed at the micro level (the words of Shawn who changed himself as an individual) as well as the macro level (Jim's description of the shearers who are freed to be more child-centered). Some men have to make choices that are difficult because of the culture (like Vineet); for others a changing society makes it easier.

The common theme is that these men choose what they believe in and maintain their integrity in doing so. Whatever the reason, the change appears to be real and, as a theorist named Robert Frank suggests, might even have survival value for the culture.[4]

In addition, the culture and the individual often evolve simultaneously. Jim summarized his own efforts when he said the following:

I try very hard not to be the strong silent type and guess I've always been an independent thinker. In my role as a father I try to show love, warmth and support to my children and my wife. The support is verbal and physical—there's a lot of hugging in this family. I don't have as much time with the children as I would like because I run a fairly large farming operation. But I try to play games with them—whatever the season is, the sport—and I read to them a lot. I hope the children will remember me as someone who really did love them and showed them I loved them.

For my wife Christobel I try to show love by doing things that show affection. I try to be concerned about what she does, aware of her needs to fulfill her life, recognize her aspirations and help her achieve them. Unfortunately I often fall short and sometimes things get lost in the translation. But to me, love is doing things that show your affection and helping that person to be happy.

Behavior, then, for men who believe in love is a mirror that reflects emotions, values, beliefs and intent. It also shines with integrity.

SUMMARY

The relationship between behavior and choice is reviewed in the chapter. Men share stories of personal journey and decision related to why they have chosen the paths they have taken. Some of the recurrent ideas are listed below.

1. Behavior is a manifestation of and mirror for integrity in men who believe in love. They understand their own feelings, thoughts and values and act on them in a consistent way.

2. They accept the importance of feelings—their own and others'.

3. They risk emotional expression and reach out to those they love.

4. They define themselves as individuals and maintain an inner standard of behavior, trying to see themselves as the kind of men they want to be.

5. They make themselves available to loved ones, persist in problem solving and hold on.

6.   They understand barnacle love.

barnacle love

imagine
a barnacle
love

a love of tenacity
that holds vise-hard
with teeth that dig neath the surface
to grip
each atom.
the barnacle is not beauteous —
it is hard-shelled
tough
and tender inside;
it endures salt water
freezing cold
wild wind
and the seductive power of waves.

when all else have gone
it is the barnacle
that remains
with the sea piling.[5]

ON A PERSONAL NOTE

We are not accustomed to recognizing behavioral intelligence. Maybe in athletic competition, perhaps, or in professional dance. However, acting in positive ways is one way of giving. When men do so—whether as father, husband, loved one, professional or more broadly as a human being—they touch others with love.

8 Mental Images: Pictures within the Mind

I suppose that in the forty-five years of my existence every atom, every molecule that composes me has changed its position or danced away and beyond to become part of other things. New molecules have come from the grass and the bodies of animals to be part of me a little while, yet in this spinning, light and airy as a midge swarm in a shaft of sunlight, my memories hold, and a beloved face of twenty years ago is before me still. Nor is that face, nor all my years, caught cellularly as in some cold, precise photographic pattern, some gross, mechanical reproduction of the past. My memory holds the past and yet paradoxically knows, at the same time, that the past is gone and will never come again. It cherishes dead faces and silenced voices, yes, and lost evenings of childhood. In some odd nonspatial way it contains houses and rooms that have been torn timber from timber and brick from brick. These have a greater permanence in that midge dance which contains them than ever they had in the world of reality.[1]

Loren Eiseley's description conveys the strength of memory and visual thinking. Eiseley, a well-known naturalist, wrote that after twenty years he could recall with vivid detail the face, voice, and perhaps even fragrance associated with a loved one. The process, far from mechanistic, involves the "subtle essences of memory, delight, and wistfulness moving among the thin wires of my brain." His mind thinks in pictures as well as thoughts.

The human brain has two hemispheres—a right and a left—which function somewhat differently. The left is associated with logic and linear thinking; the right with visual thinking and creativity. The hemispheres operate separately and interactively. While some of the research in this area is fascinating, it is beyond the scope of that which can be shared here.

We are, however, interested in how mental imagery affects people in general and men specifically, and how it influences their behavior. The stories of the men in this section support the observation made by Loren Eiseley: visual thinking and memory are powerful. Men who believe in love are able to develop and maintain positive images of love and of women.

IMAGES FROM THE PAST

Some images from the past are as vivid as if they were imprinted in wet concrete. Years later attempts to access these deep, crevasse-like impressions brings them to the surface with all the sensory detail of a leaf which, having fallen into prehistoric mud, yields a fossil in which even the veins can be seen clearly. While there is much research on why memories decay and fade, it also has been recognized that memory retention is affected by a variety of situational and individual factors.

Remember the house you grew up in or your first childhood sweetheart? Such memories may have been strongly encoded or stored because, among other things, they had strong emotion associated with them; they occurred during a time when the neural system was particularly responsive to neurochemical memory mapping; they were stored in a multisensory manner. Many different factors can enhance or inhibit the ability to access clearly images from the past. In this respect and in many other cognitive ways, people are different. Nevertheless, some of the men whose stories are shared in this section recall similar experiences with images and emotion.

Eric Gavin

Eric, a twenty-nine year old self-employed general contractor, is a native of Jersey City, New Jersey. His work requires good visual-spatial skills, and he has a strong artistic side to his personality. An attractive man, he has been married eight years to his wife Denise. He reflected on four different types of images during our interview. Some of them are rooted in the past, others in the present.

Images of Men (Present): I don't think of men as different from women because I view every guy as an individual. How do I view myself as a man? I see myself as loving, at peace, still hard-working (you can't help that) and nonjudgmental. I picture myself as a man being self-sacrificing for my family and not selfish.

Images of Love for my Wife (Present): I think of a song. There is a song by The Police called "Every Little Thing She Does Is Magic" which I think of, but there are different songs on different occasions. That particular song always reminds me of the fun we have together. We have more fun now than we've ever had before, even with all the hard work in building our house (which I'm doing myself). We just laugh.

My mother and her boyfriend were visiting recently and she said, "I've never seen two married people laugh so much—every time I'm with you guys, it always amazes me."

And here we are, in a co-op we paid $45,000 for, which is currently selling for $3,000 and we don't let it bring us down. I think it's because I trust her; I trust that she's not going to bail out no matter how bad it gets. I'm not afraid when it gets bad because I know it will get better. And I know she will be there.

In this image, then, Eric sees them laughing, having fun, and together. The trust he feels is partly a function of seeing Denise in the picture as she always has been—beside him. However, it was not easy for him to get to know her initially.

Image from the Past: The First Time I Saw Her: When I first met Denise she was dressed in man's clothes. She looked great. She was a waitress, wore black slacks, a white tuxedo shirt and black bow tie. She had long, long hair. I was a customer at the restaurant, I was with someone else, but I decided to take a chance. She was so beautiful I felt out of my league but in a gambling mood. The group I was with was leaving, but I pretended I forgot something and went back into the restaurant. I asked her for her phone number and she said, "No."

My grandmother was one of the people in the group and she knew I liked that waitress. A week or two later she went back into the restaurant and told Denise that her grandson wanted to call her. Denise remembered that my grandmother had been with the group and gave her the phone number. We were both 21. We married within a year. I can still picture every detail of how she looked at that restaurant. I think of it often.

Eric was impressed by Denise but somewhat apprehensive, too. Excitement and fear were part of the imprinting process as well as visual beauty. In addition, his artistic nature paid attention to small visual detail, and his sincerity impressed a bystander, his grandmother.

Images of Marriage: There is something I wrote once for a friend's wedding. I was the best man and I read it as part of the toast at the reception. It is the picture I have of a marriage— at least the way it should be—and it is how I see my own.

> We could think of a marriage as a house, with many rooms:
> a room for Understanding
> a room for Trust
> a room for Patience
> a room for Planning the Future,
> and a room for Solitude as well as
> one for Passion and Love.
> (Also, there should be at least two bathrooms.)
> Our house can withstand any Storm, for its foundation is
> built on Friendship.

In many ways, Eric's images—past, present and projected into the future—blend together. He sees men in terms of how he sees himself, as an individual. And the mental pictures of his wife Denise increase feelings of love and commitment. Mental images are related to behavior in a symbolic way.

When you look at a scene, you respond on two levels. The first is in terms of the current picture. The second is the mental image evoked, perhaps a memory with emotional significance. The visual similarity between the two scenes may be slight, but you process and respond to both the present image and the mental image. An example may make this clearer.

A man sees his wife working in the garden (the current picture) and is reminded of the first time he saw her (the mental image evoked by the current picture). Maybe the visual similarity between the two scenes is simply the way she has fixed her hair. The man responds by going over and kissing her—partly because of the present (gardening) and partly because of the past (the mental image of their first meeting). The two images are being processed simultaneously with the man responding to both.

Mental images may affect behavior, then, in the following way.

```
stimulus situation>                    >man's behavior
    (wife gardening) I              I (kisses her)
                      I       I
                      V
          Image of actual scene (gardening)
    Mental image from past (symbolic—when he first saw her)
```

The remaining stories in this chapter reflect a variety of images of women, love and relationships. What is significant is the degree to which these men have, in spite of the barrage of negative images of women reflected in the media, managed to retain positive mental images of women. Such images, then, translate into behavior that is positive. Likewise, as images change, behavior changes.

Ard Erickson

Ard Erickson is a Norwegian businessman who works in international finance and lives in New York. An MBA who is highly successful in his field, Ard describes the change in his mental pictures over the course of his life.

From the time I was young, my father was away from home. As a result, I took over the role of the man of the family, and while many of my friends were out playing, my childhood from age nine on was filled with much work. I had to finish my tasks before I could go play. I learned early the responsibility of working and taking charge of my own life, not relying on other people to prepare things for me.

I grew up in a blue-collar family—very few people had a university education. What people really valued was to start your own business and build something from scratch. I imagined life as work—and participating in the outdoors: fishing, hunting, skiing, sailing.

My image of *life as work* changed, partly as a result of travel. Extensive travel in the United States and most of Europe has helped me to expand my view. As you get to know people raised in different settings, you can compare how you were raised. And you can add what you like about other cultures and shed what you don't like about yours, but you always keep your roots.

From the French and the Belgians I came to a new understanding of the importance of good food and its preparation. With a Norwegian upbringing, a few times a year—during the holidays—you put your heart into good food. The rest of the time the purpose of food was to fill the stomach and make you healthy. From the French, I could see that you don't have to eat mediocre meals. And the meal was viewed as a point of relaxation, something to enjoy as well as the company. This was lacking in the Norwegian culture, where a business lunch was half an hour and you would wolf down your food so you could get back to work. There is no Norwegian lunch culture; lunch only interrupts work. Then you go home and work on your house—leaving work only means going off to start work again.

My home life has been the other half of my mental picture of life that has changed. My wife grew up in Italy. From her I have learned to play and to relax. She has taught me that life is about fun, not work. And my daughter helps me in the garage and we play. This is a very different picture from the one I grew up with and it has changed the way I live.

Ard describes the imprinting of one image—work—by his culture and early life experience. When his father was away, Ard, as the boy, had to fill in and do the man's work around the house and yard. After school, he was often working. The image that imprinted reflected a concept of life defined by effort and unpleasant but necessary tasks. As he grew, that image changed in two ways.

First, traveling provided alternate images of what life could be like. The French and Belgians, in particular, took an old functional picture (eating) and presented a new perspective. Ard expanded his mental image, correspondingly, to include the new one.

Second, the culture of his wife Stephanie and her philosophy of life differed from his own. She was more fun-loving and playful. She viewed the family as a group of people who could enjoy themselves together as well as provide mutual support. The vivid colors of her world splashed over into his and added a dimension to home similar to that he experienced when closely connected to nature. The feeling of being alive had been brightened and expanded. Ard chose to incorporate both of these changes into his life.

You learn to adapt. What I learned as I got older was to express my feelings a bit more and to let go of some of the boundaries that were restricting or confining. It's a slow process of development that takes place over time and happens through being exposed to and watching others you can learn from. Over time you find yourself daring to behave in the way you feel comfortable even if that is the way people don't expect you to. That probably is the secret of happiness—you behave in co-ordination with your feelings, even if that is against the restrictions that were put on you in your culture.

Images from the past, then, can remain. They can also be changed. Negative ones can be replaced or expanded into positive ones, and men can learn from alternate images, whether provided by a different culture or a woman he loves. He can recognize that it is he who ultimately defines his own psychological boundaries. This is choice at the micro and macro level. Here Ard is choosing an image which has a powerful effect.

IMAGES AND SELF-AWARENESS

There is no substitute for self-awareness. It is essentially a type of intelligence, although we don't classify it as such. Some individuals have the ability to stand back and observe themselves objectively. Self-awareness is learned and shows in your relationship with the self, which directly affects others. Self-awareness can be captured in mental images, as is apparent in some of the comments that follow from men whose stories appeared earlier in the book.

Jim Anderson

Jim, the Australian whose comments appeared in Chapter 7, shared the following image on love related to his children.

> I know it's a cliché, but you think it's impossible to love anything as much as you do your children. When I pick up the boys at night to take them to the bathroom—walk past the bathroom mirror and see this small smiling child in my arms—it is just a wonderful feeling.

His is a beautiful image with a sense of self-awareness. How many parents might walk by, not noticing the picture in the mirror and not acknowledging their own vulnerability to feeling?

Larry

Larry, an American whose interview appears in Chapter 6, shared the following image of love with a woman.

> To me love is a powerful feeling similar to a mystery novel that never has a solution. It just intertwines us deeper and deeper becoming more complex as the involvement and commitment become stronger. It means that I will need to continue to grow in understanding throughout my life and relationship.

Larry pictures love as a challenge, a winding path of understanding that might never be fully explored. This mental image places him in a position of humility as well as discovery.

Per Bjarte

Per Bjarte, a Norwegian, tells his story in Chapter 7. His image of women is shared here.

> I see women as partners and relationships with women as a partnership. A great deal is shared in Norway. In the last 20–30 years, women have become very active in many arenas. From the local community to the government level and in all political systems they are involved. We have more female ministers than male ministers, for example, and we have had a female Prime Minister for several years.
>
> There are, however, some people who have retained a different view of women, one carried over from their parents when they were young. Generally women are viewed as equal and relationships are seen as partnerships. The man may tend to do more of the machinery work and cut the

grass; the woman may spend more time with the children. Partners don't have to do identical tasks; they just need to be valued equally.

Per Bjarte commented on the degree to which he tries to share parenting and his views of equity related to worth. Money is not how he values people and his partnership with his wife is one in which respect is mutual. Respect for another comes from a sense of worth for that person—and one that can be reflected in a mental image.

Hans Krichels

Hans is a Maine writer. Images from his story "Snowbound" reflect his view of love.

. . . In the middle of nowhere now, the man sits at his octagonal table. He seems fascinated by the light & dark, the demarcation; it *must* be important; there are so many other things he could be doing with his time. He could be ruing the coldness of his life at the moment, crying for his lost children, yearning for the love and laughter he'd found one time or another, fuming over one betrayal or another. But he's done all that before, and it seems unimportant to him now. Instead, he contemplates the line. He is *not* unhappy; he smiles inwardly, chuckles to himself, continues flipping through the pages of his journal.

Feb. 4—The woodpeckers are back at my feeder this morning, a pair of harries, proud and distinguished. The male, with his red splash of color (red as roses, red as blood in the snow), reminds me of a retired bullfighter. I call him Boris. Carlotta, the female, still makes occasional guest appearances on stages around the world. Together, they make a striking couple. This is a third mating for both of them, and they are wise and philosophical about their lives. In the course of my lengthy discussions with them, I've learned a great deal about aloneness and courage, about love and laughter and life.

"For all of that," Boris announced this morning, "to live

without love is like getting your beak stuck in a fencepost that's more rotten than you thought it was."

Feb. 11—In your letter today, you wrote about love, about the courage it takes to love fully. You wrote about the "new school," a phenomenon of our age, you called it, the anti-lovers, the growing legions of wounded people, afraid to love, making a virtue of self-control, self-preservation. "Why do you *need* love?" they ask the lovers, as if love itself were a weakness, an addiction.

April 23—The ice is gone from the pond this morning. I stood on the shore throwing pebbles into the black glassy water, watching the circles radiate outward. And I thought about this business of love, how it's like those circles if it's to be true and real at all. At the center, of course, you must love yourself. Without that, there can be no radiant energy. With it, you can then love the world around you in ever-widening circles. Ideally, of course, at the center, you will find a compatible soul for the giving and the gathering of the most intimate love. Perhaps that's not necessary—Boris and his rotten fencepost notwithstanding.

The man is chuckling again now. In the end, there is a *reason* he is not unhappy. For all the harsh simplicity of the line, its cold geometry and logical perfection, its absolutes and its various delineations—all of which the man *will* come to grips with—what the man is really contemplating is something beyond the line. And it is the love, of course, the love he has shared, that brings him back to the concentricity and circularity of his life.

In the end, the line tells nothing; night will always give way to the day; the earth will circle the sun; sunlight will sparkle on the snow, thawing, bringing life to the crocuses and daffodils—on and on, in endless cycles.

The warmth of the sun, the colors of the flowers. . . . Snowbound, in the middle of nowhere, the man feels the warmth at the heart of the storm. "Love is real," he writes in his journal. Then absentmindedly, he adds, "I love, that's all, I just love." Before scrawling, almost illegibly, "But I miss you." Obviously, the man has not lost hope. Snowbound, he moves from his octagonal table—something about the dark geometry against the whiteness of the wall. . . .[2]

In the excerpt from his story, Hans shares several images. Through the writer's pen we see pain in the lost children, self-reflection in the glassy water and a sense of peace in the cyclical nature of things. The endless cycles imply another chance at love which offers a source of hope. He can walk away from the octagonal table because he knows he can return to it. "I love," he writes . . . [(therefore) I hope].

Anthony St. John

Anthony St. John is British, forty-four years old. He lives in London. He describes himself and his family of origin as very open and good at expressing their feelings.

> We are so open, we are almost un-British. If someone looks pretty or the meal is good, we say it. Our family is very open and loving. Because of the contrast with the culture as the British are slightly reserved, we tend to stand out. But I am actually modest.
>
> I have always been open to emotion and to love as a part of emotion. I grew up with two sisters and always had strong heterosexual emotion. I fell in love all the time. I can remember each relationship of my life very clearly, and it was love from Day One.
>
> My first love was when I was thirteen—it was real. I ran all the way from my house—miles—just to touch her, just to hold her hand. Her name was Susan.
>
> Love is when you're with and enjoy the company of someone absolutely. It drives away distractions and negatives (the "shouldn't do" and "shouldn't be"). When I met my wife I fell in love instantly, it was like the culmination of all the previous times. I knew instantly this was the absolute. I would have married her the next day, and I had had no intention of getting married. Love to me didn't mean marriage; it just meant love. We waited three months. By other people's standards it was terribly short, but for us it was long.

What place do I see love as having in my life? I suppose that sort of ultimate bonding strengthens everything. Up until I met her I was very casual about money, responsibilities, friendships, but that bonding or teaming sort of pulls all the loose ends together. I don't like the idea of homebuilding (nesting) but you develop a sort of joint life. I never thought I'd do that.

In the early days love and lust sort of went hand-in-hand. I didn't realize that there was that much more.

Eagles, you know, mate for life. My parents are like that. They are still married, very old, but through all the problems they stayed together for life.

My philosophy of life? I don't know. I think belief in love maximizes honesty.

Anthony, in his comments about himself and his view of love, echoes some of the elements of "Snowbound." He accepts his feelings as real; allows himself to risk love as a natural part of self-expression; and becomes intensely affected by those women whose lives have touched his. His sense of himself as a man and his image of himself as a lover are congruent.

At the same time, Anthony and "Snowbound" are different. "Snowbound" revolves around depth, is reflective and meditative. Anthony is spontaneous. "Snowbound" is about creating the image; Anthony is the fun and spontaneity that follows based on that image. He was, from a young age and still is intense, passionate, open—and, like many of the men whose stories appear on these pages, an eagle.

Once in a while an eagle

Once in a while comes an eagle—
an eagle so noble
it fills the sky
and flies high above the rest
with a grandeur of soul
that glides on lift
and floats
silent.

> *among people such ones are rare—*
> *in a lifetime,*
> *maybe two or three—*
> *but they change you*
> *forever.*[3]

IMAGES OF HOPES, DREAMS AND WISDOM

If imagery is such a powerful vehicle for thought, it certainly must have been harnessed as a resource for psychological change. Actually, many writers have attempted to do just that. Imagery processes have been utilized successfully in training athletes to excel and in teaching self-help skills. One of the best books in the field is one by Dr. Arnold Lazarus called *In the Mind's Eye*. How mental imagery intertwines with words and actions is presented by Dr. Lazarus in several of his other works.[4]

Daniel Merriam

Daniel is a thirty-one year old artist, a single man, who lives in Florida. Daniel's work has been cited as having a spontaneous, dreamlike quality. He was interviewed because, at a fundamental level, as an artist and a person, he believes in love.

I define love in terms of creative power; giving it to someone makes you see the empowerment of it. When you get it, you see the energy again. Art is probably a vehicle in which to express love. It requires a certain passion and intention. As long as art exists, it continues to radiate love.

What actually motivates art can't be money, which is not inspiring in a multidimensional manner; money inspires in only a linear way. Love is multidimensional—it has many moving parts within it that work in combination to create energy.

Love cannot be measured or completely explained. It comes out in ways that almost seem magical. I think love is a very pure feeling.

The only thing that can be compared to art would be nature—a place you can find inspiration for art. I think nature helps you understand the importance of your feelings and your honesty. You can't deny the reality of nature, but you can deny your own inner nature, which leads to loss of compassion.

My paintings are a manuscript of my feelings and thoughts. Some of my recent work focused on a relationship as it rose and fell. I used one type of love (my art) to get through the pain of another type of love (the loss of a relationship). It was healing to my heart and got me through a difficult time.

Daniel describes how he sees the relationship between love and art in his life. He also expresses how he uses the love that motivates his art to help him heal emotional pain. What the relationship took away (the loss of love), the process of his art restored (the return of love). Artistic vision provides an alternate view of the world.

Image of a man open to love: When a man opens his heart to his own inner love, I think of this as turning yourself inside out so your insides are exposed. Let's say you're a cabinet and you have hanging on hooks things like whistles, bells, trinkets. You open all the doors on your cabinet and show what is there—that's symbolic of being open to your own feelings.

Image of a woman I love: I have all my guards down and am able to think thoughts and share them. It's not keeping secrets about who you are and how you feel. I think of it as when you're lying beside someone and you're at your peak point, you kind of meld together like two people sharing the same body—two brains working together, you share each other's trust. As much as you trust your own mind, you have two brains that could work together.

Image of the world: I think there is a love network, a group of people who believe in love and recognize others who do as well. They choose specifically to trust and to associate and even do business with them. They recognize others who choose love as a way of life and a way of thinking.

Image of love: Love is energy that rekindles the other as well as the self.

Why do I believe in love? Because it works. Of all the concepts I've known in my life, the only one that has stayed true to me is love. I learned this from people who knew the power of love and shared it with me. They saw some innate goodness in me and cultivated it. I also experienced it from my art. What I put into my art and what it gives back to me is love.

Daniel's verbal images are like his visual ones—strong. One of his paintings, called *Number 13*, depicts a piranha, jaws extended, ready to bite down on a heart. Striking contrast, the harshness of malice with the softness of the apple-like heart.

Artistic vision is a type of conceptual leadership. Historically, artists were able to communicate with the masses in ways that freed certain types of expression. The French Impressionists, for example, led a movement in art whose impact is still felt today. Their work was nonverbal, composed of images of light. One striking example of the artist as conceptual leader, bringing a vision to life, is Claude Monet. Not only did he paint the gardens of Giverny; he built them! He pictured a scene of overwhelming beauty, built it and then captured it on canvas, where it has remained.

In a sense, Daniel's image of a network of people who believe in love is like Monet's vision of the garden. He has recognized a beautiful potentiality which at the present time remains unbuilt. As an artist, he acknowledges dreams. And while I would not have thought along these lines, particularly in terms of people doing business with others based on goodness, I have done just that in my practice. I take seriously my responsibility for my patients, and when I need to refer them for any professional service—whether the referral they need is medical, legal, psychiatric, or instructional—I tend to use personal as well as professional criteria in selecting the referral. Unlike the old boys' network, this referral system is based on professional training as well as personal goodness. At the end of the line, I know my patients will receive good service and be cared about as individuals. On a small scale, then, the network Daniel envisions is already in operation. In the next story, a man finds himself in something similar.

Jerry Vigna

A native of Philadelphia, Jerry is a writer, teacher and theologian. Happily married for fifteen years, his comments come from an essay he wrote entitled *Episodes in Loving and Being Loved*.

This is a funny place to begin. I am rigorously logical and I wear like a medal having once been designated a "cold-blooded rationalist" by one of my staff. I'm not like that, really. So when I was asked to pull together my thoughts on love, my left brain reached for something systematic (whether philosophy, religion or social science—it didn't matter) and my right brain said, "You can't capture it that way!" A series of illustrations, most of them recent experiences, came to mind.

Love Returns and Flows Out Again
Jim lost his job last year. After eighteen years with a single organization, doing a job that exists in fewer than a dozen companies in the country, he had to start over. He will never have that job again.

I'm a veteran of job-hunting wars. Years ago I paid cash for one of those services that promises to help you uncover the hidden job market and get the really good jobs. I'm not cowed by the need to search for work, so I cornered Jim at a church function and with cool logic gave him the names of former bosses and clients and some advice on networking.

I didn't even like him at the time, but remembering the help others had given me, I chose to return the good deed. Now I'm out of work, and it was Jim who gave me a refresher course on those job-hunting techniques and names of some colleagues.

We've also gotten to know each other better over the past several months. He's not so bad—insightful and pleasant, actually.

Angels

Jennifer showed up at the company banquet. I was beside myself, having just been informed I was the only person in the company who wasn't getting a bonus. Jen and I worked together for more than a year until she went on maternity leave a few months before the annual dinner. By the end of the night, I was in the bar, drinking and crying like a baby. Suddenly and unexpectedly, she opened a door. Revealing a few secrets she didn't have to and giving me a few names to call, she put the pieces back together. A sudden, quick message brought hope and comfort, both delivered in a most ordinary way.

That's how it is with angels. They come and go, and leave you thankful for the love you received. I can't explain to you how that was anything more than a conversation between two friends and former co-workers in a bar, but it was.

Love and Family

On May 10, 1968, Pat and I exchanged names and fell in love. We were at the junior prom with different dates when we introduced ourselves to each other. That quickly, we were in love and have been ever since. Not that we married immediately after high school. We spent six years debating each other's lifestyle. Neither of us saw the sense in becoming serious about someone so different. Finally, on May 19, 1974, we fell into each other's arms, exhausted.

Our marriage has had all the ups and downs of any marriage. Our two children have made greater that mystical feeling that pervades this household, even the greatest uncertainties, such as wondering where the money will come from, melt away when we're together.

This is really the hardest form of love to describe. Love is the ground of being, and in its strongest manifestation, ineffable. When I imagine their absence, I have no words. Instead, I see, and my vision is of the blackest night.

So?
Love comes in many shapes and sizes. It is social and an act of friendship. It is also communal and protective. It is part of every aspect of living a life that has any satisfaction whatsoever. Without it, I just wouldn't be having much fun.

Love provides more than enjoyment, however. It is a principle I can stand up for. It is a way that I can choose to live my life. But it isn't just something to think about. It's something to feel and do.[5]

Jerry's comments are of interest for several reasons. Considering he has a Ph.D. in theology and is adept at logical analysis, his introductory comments "You can't capture it (love) that way" are especially telling. He echoes some of the philosophy mentioned by Floyd Thompkins earlier, that "truth is something beyond just the facts." You might capture love, but not in a linear way.

His image of angels, theology aside, seems congruent with the sentiments expressed by other men within the context of this book. Daniel recalled good people aiding other good people and said that he himself had so benefited. Eric was aided by his grandmother who helped him obtain the phone number of his future wife. In David's story other people served as psychological supports. In Chapter 5 William Gipson reported how influential relationships with his male college peers freed his capacity to love women. The intimacy they shared and the positive influence they provided made a difference in his life. Whatever the descriptor, people with a high GQ (goodness quotient) are partly responsible for increasing the common good.

Goodness and social contribution is important in the eyes of the next man. He is a well-known teacher, psychologist, and author. He and his wife established the Gilbert and Kathleen Wrenn Humanitarian and Caring Person Award within the American Counseling Association (formerly the American Personnel and Guidance Association). Their strong commitment to encouraging the development of kindness within the professional counseling community is symbolized by the yearly award of one thousand dollars.

C. Gilbert Wrenn

C. Gilbert Wrenn, currently Professor Emeritus in Counseling Psychology at Arizona State University, has taught extensively abroad and at some twenty universities. He has been a prolific author or co-author of textbooks and personal development books; has contributed chapters in the books of other writers; and has published hundreds of journal articles. Past President of three national personnel organizations, he has received eighteen awards and citations including the Bronze Star Medal, Honorary Litt. D. and Fulbright Distinguished Scholar Award.

Gilbert was my first mentor. In my professional life, I have been fortunate enough to have two mentors, and while they are very different from each other, both are individuals of exceptional integrity as well as accomplishment. Both have been leaders in the area of emotional healing, and what I learned from them has changed my life. They were and are men whose superior intelligence is matched by an equally superior goodness (GQ).

I remember the first time I met Dr. Wrenn. I had read one of his books and knew he would be a wonderful mentor. I chose him because, in addition to his professional expertise, I sensed he was at a high level of moral development. Although these things are very difficult to measure, I wanted to grow in that direction.

I was a doctoral student at the time and wanted to schedule an appointment with Dr. Wrenn. The department secretary told me that he scheduled his own appointments so I waited outside his office until he was scheduled to appear.

"I would like to make an appointment with you," I said.

"For what reason?" he asked.

"I would like to ask you to be my mentor."

"Well," he replied. "That's not exactly how these things are done. Usually it is the mentor who, becoming aware of the student's work, extends the invitation."

"Oh," I said. "I didn't know that. I have read your work and know that I could learn much from you. I would value it highly if we could consider an alternative."

A very busy man with many professional responsibilities, he ended up giving me his time. We developed an informal mentoring relationship, as he was getting ready to retire. We published a book review together, and he has been a source of learning and inspiration for me ever since. He is, in a sense, in my own goodness network.

Gilbert and his wife Kathleen, a musician and teacher, have been married for sixty-eight "very good" years. Their story appears below in Gilbert's words.

Our marriage was sixty-eight years old on June 15, 1994. Kathleen and I started out with a love affair and are winding up that way. Our romance developed over the years to a growing respect, each for the other one. Respect joined romance through the many intense and varied experiences over these several decades. Kathleen has become more than my mate; she is a distinct person of artistic sensitivity, of integrity, of compassion for others—and I am an important one of the "others"! Her honesty sometimes stings, but her compassion, her acts of love for me as a Person, make the "sting" just that, no more. It makes me look at myself and profit from Kathleen's different way of looking at life. If I respect her, I respect her differences, learn from them.

Toleration of the other person's differences is not enough; one *accepts* those differences as meaningful to each of us. If

I love her, I must remember that she accepts in me some differences in behavior, in attitudes that are strange to her. She accepts them in me as part of the Person she loves and respects. Kathleen once paid me a high compliment when she said, "You know, dear, you are not just my husband, you are my best friend."

Yes, there is Hope for Love if each adds respect for the other, gained over years of accepting the other's differences.

Each person is a wondrous creation if each looks for the wonder in the other and *accepts* the other's differences as appropriate to that Person.

Gilbert Wrenn sees him and his wife as different and acceptance of the differences as critical for the maintenance of a good relationship. He is a scientist; she is a musician. Their backgrounds are in different worlds; the bridge across them is acceptance of difference and love.

They have always reminded me of the couple from mythology: Baucis and Philemon, a story outlined in *Bullfinch's Mythology*, which I remember reading in the eighth grade.[6] In ancient times Jupiter, king of the gods, was visiting earth in human form. Accompanying him, also in disguised form, was his son Mercury. The two stopped at each home along the road, asking for rest and refreshment. Everyone turned them away, everyone except Baucis and Philemon.

The elderly couple, married in youth, had grown old together. Neither wealthy nor elite, they welcomed the weary travelers and shared with them their humble home, making a warm meal and treating them kindly. The guests, being supernatural beings, replenished the wine and food, much to the surprise of their hosts. Eventually, the hosts discovered the identity of their guests. Falling on their knees in humility, the couple were ashamed they had so little to offer the celestial beings. Asking them to rise, Jupiter and Mercury told them they would be rewarded.

The remainder of the town sank into a lake, punishment for their cruel rejection of the weary travelers. The home of the elderly couple was transformed into a temple, and they were told that the gods would grant one wish. It was the husband Philemon who spoke. "Since we have lived our entire lives in love and harmony, we ask that we die together." The couple maintained the temple until their last day when, instead of dying, each was turned into a tree whose trunks wound around the other. The trees are there still, legend had it, on a ridge in Phrygia—a tribute to eternal love.

SUMMARY

Within the chapter are shared stories of men reflecting images of love. Mental pictures related to the overlap of the past, present, and future are presented as well as those which show internal psychological change. Some of the major points are outlined below.

1. Mental imagery is powerful. It reflects a mental process that has an effect on behavior and is influenced by it.

2. Men who believe in love have managed to develop and retain healthy self-images in spite of negative experiences.

3. To more clearly understand men's behavior toward women, we must more clearly understand the mental images they act on—the pictures of women retained within the mind.

4. Men who believe in love manage to retain positive mental images of women, in spite of those to the contrary portrayed by the culture.

5. Men who believe in love accept their own emotional vulnerability. They act on that vulnerability, integrate new learning experiences within it and choose ways to cope that do not imprison the hearts in armour.

6. Hope for love is maintained; a belief in goodness validated; and fun appreciated in men whose belief and imagery system includes love.

ON A PERSONAL NOTE

Images of love are treasures. Some of them are visual and others are sensory impressions, stored within our mental library. As children we often sensed love. Some people we were drawn to; others, we withdrew from. Memories of those who warmed us were mentally stored in pictures, conversations, aromas, tastes and touch. Each of us has a library of love.

Hold on to this library and add to it. Become increasingly aware of the sensory ways of knowing which are so uniquely personal. Not only great artists have the ability to create pictures; each of us can do so to different degrees within the mind. Nurture this ability. It allows the beauty of life and love to remain more alive—in daily activities and within the rich journal of your personal history. As such, you do what physics cannot—discover that which transcends time. It is love.

> *Mirror Man*:
> *For Doug*
>
> *If I were nine and you were sixteen*
>   *you'd be the boy I'd want to marry*
>   *when I grew up.*
>
> *If I were thirty and you were three*
>   *you'd be the son I'd want to have*
>   *someday.*
>
> *If I were six and you were eight*
>   *you'd be the brother I always wanted—*
>   *another kid to explore with.*
>
> *If I were sixteen and you were forty*
>   *you'd be the father I always wanted*
>   *someone*
>   *to believe in me.*

If you were woman and I was man
  you'd be the mother, nurturing
    the child in me.

Funny, the paradox stands.
  you are none—
    yet all.

You live in my loving soul
  kin in my heart of
    real love.[7]

PART FOUR

Moving into Love

9 Where Do We Go from Here?

Love is one of the most important things in the world. It is, as several men have shared, one of the most powerful. Its beacon shines in the four corners of the world. Men who do not know each other, living in different parts of the globe, report on its light in their lives.

Our journey toward love has taken us into the hearts of these men. We have traveled through the lives of men who love and entered into the realm of love itself. We have learned that part of this territory is known and part is yet uncharted. That which is known is perhaps the smallest part, and some of our conceptual maps don't work as well as they should when we are in the process of discovery.

Understanding people is difficult. So is understanding love. Both are highly complex. Here we have relied partly on personal experience; partly on the stories of the men; partly on our own intuitive sense of the loving territory to be explored. As scientists of human nature we wish to understand; as artists of our own lives we want to add more brilliance to the inner depths of ourselves and those important to us.

The challenges of understanding men who believe in love and love itself place us in a humbling position. We are, in a sense, like scientists facing a new phenomenon or studying something that is not behaving the way the laws of physics predict it should behave. When that happens, scientists evoke what is called the "willing suspension of disbelief." They admit they don't necessarily understand all the aspects of what they are observing, but because they determine it to be important, they suspend judgment and wait and see what happens. They persist in learning more.

We are in a similar position when trying to understand the vastness of love and the magnitude of the importance of men who champion love—whether they do so in the world or within the circle of their own lives. We can rely somewhat on science, but we might do better to suspend disbelief and just watch. In the arena of love, science has more to learn, as the next story illustrates.

A SCIENTIST LOOKS AT LOVE

"My degree is in biochemistry and I worked in research laboratories from age seventeen on. For the past ten years I have worked in management. I am foremost a scientist."

The speaker is John Carter, Ph.D., who grew up in London and now lives in the United States.

> My story, I suppose, is somewhat unusual although it didn't start out that way. I grew up in a caring English family; played cricket as a young man and was active in the Boy Scouts as well as my church—the Anglican Church. I was responsible, chosen for leadership, and as patrol leader in the Scouts was often expected to successfully return other Scouts to safety from survival camping trips such as in the mountains of Wales. I saw myself as somewhat of a leader and adventurer. On other trips, some of the kids who were my age, between nine and eleven, became homesick; others were scared and crying in a tent with rain pouring in at 2 AM, while the adult leaders were at the far ends of the fields. I talked the kids through it and developed another component to my personality—a sensitivity to the feelings of others and a sense of nurturing.
>
> At sixteen I would accompany my father to the pub, evidence of the transition from childhood into being a man. Growing up, I had few girlfriends I was extremely fond of and did well in school. Education was always at the fore-

front of my goals, and I thought at one point about being a physician. I decided to pursue scientific research. The work enabled me to support myself and gain experience in the scientific world while I continued my studies. I had defined myself as a scholar, yet another component of my personality—perhaps the largest part. It was at this point that my story diverges.

When I first married, my wife and I were considered the perfect couple. I loved her, we never argued, and our relationship was viewed as ideal. I never thought of words like respect or intensity; we were just developing a life together. Then all that changed.

We had gone to a Halloween party. The party was crowded—there were twenty-four people in one room—and as I looked around, I saw Diana, who was with her husband. We looked across the room at each other and in that absolute instant, two marriages came to a screeching halt and a third one was born. I knew at the end of the evening something had happened that could not be quantified.

I am a scientist, I don't believe in this stuff—the ultimate in an emotional experience. If you can't prove it, I have difficulty accepting it. But here was my life, totally changed, in an instant.

For the next nine months I tried to understand what had happened. Over time, the couples separated and then our relationship took off. The relationship with Diana grew and even today, after twenty-four years of marriage, when you talk about love and emotions, it is something the likes of which I don't think I've seen in another couple. The intensity and power of the emotion and passion we share takes us to a different plane of experience and discovery. It is something beyond words—beyond understanding.

There was basically nothing wrong with my first marriage—nothing wrong with her marriage—this was instantaneous.

I've allowed love to be an important part of my identity. I've been with Diana for twenty-four years, and demonstrating that love is foremost in my life. In my early years the focus was on education. My career growth has been consistent and I am highly regarded in my field. Two concentric circles define my life: love and work. My relationship with Diana is at the center.

I have changed a lot since I have known her and since we have been together. And from her I have learned so much. We don't lean on each other—we are simply happy to be together. The love part of the relationship is the lifeblood that keeps me going.

Sometimes, in a crowded room at a social function when each of us is talking to others, we both might happen to look up. She might catch my eye and that split moment is such pure heaven or joy. We'll leave the party and revel that we happened to look up and know the other was there. That to me is just incredible intensity of love. It is rare.

I have integrated this into my identity because it feels wonderful. So intense for us, so strong. People don't know, sometimes, that something like this is possible.

How do you keep a relationship intense like that? We have a philosophy: we will always act like we did when we first met. Working on the relationship is paramount to keeping that intensity going. I would buy flowers in those days; a gift for no reason. Or Diana might be in the next town at a business meeting, and we'll drive twenty-two miles to meet each other for lunch! We get excited to have a date with each other. Those are the things you did when you first met the other person. You maintain the romance. And it grows.

Dr. Carter captures the nonverbal component of relationships. A dimension, as he explains, beyond words. His story also presents a picture of relationships as complex with several planes of experience existing at once.

Within the framework of science, explanations of phenomena are attempted. When problems are fairly complex, additional dimensions have to be added to the analysis. Simple linear analysis is not sufficient.

Physicists and mathematicians often think in terms of multiple dimensions to solve multivariate problems. Consider, for example, an astrophysicist working on a problem in plotting the course of a satellite. Suppose the problem involved calculating when an asteroid would hit the planet Jupiter so that adjustments could be made in the course of Voyager to avoid damage. The astrophysicist might take into account several factors: gravity, satellite size, mass and velocity, to name only a few. Some of these variables are interdependent, making such analyses complex. As such, all factors would probably be included in the analysis because they could simultaneously affect the outcome. Analyzing the problem in only one parameter would result in a partial answer.

A similar position could be taken for the understanding of love. First, however, more background information is needed. In order to determine where we are going, sometimes we need to more fully understand where we've been.

SCIENCE AND LOVE

In science, a view is taken from the outside (how things appear in everyday life) and from the inside (internal composition such as molecular or atomic structure). Professor Roger Penrose, Rouse Ball Professor of Mathematics at Oxford University, is quoted in a text called *Imagined Worlds: Stories of Scientific Discovery*.[1] He explains the nature of multidimensionality in science. His discussion addresses the idea of space.

> In mathematics we often go beyond three-dimensional or even four-dimensional space, to eight, ten, a hundred or an infinite number of dimensions.... These spaces are invented basically in order to understand, get a better feeling for problems and puzzles. My own personal interest has been in spaces which have an important relevance to the physical world, and deal with the space in which we live.

In the study of love, we are not yet at the point of Professor Penrose's description. We have not quantified all the dimensions in order to more fully understand the puzzle. Moreover, we cannot be sure that love will ever lend itself to such an analysis. For fun, let's indulge ourselves in such an analysis and consider the contrast between the external and internal aspects of love.

How love appears in the minds of others—their awareness of a relationship they see—might be thought of as the external dimension. People make evaluations of someone else's relationship based on how things look from the outside. Remember the description of the pretenders in Chapter 2? Things are not always as they appear.

Within this text we explored several elements of love. Belief systems and mental images can be the results of choices one makes. Such choices are a form of behavior, but the belief systems and images themselves are sources of loving behavior. In this we see a cycle and interaction of different dimensions. Emotion is another component, as is the nonverbal.

But as all of these men have shared within the pages of this book, love is more than a science. And as at least one contemporary theorist has observed, *love is a story*.[2] Love is multifaceted—passionate love; love of life; family and agape (unselfish) love—all can coexist within the same individual. It is dynamic; it grows, changes form and affects those it comes in contact with. It is both affected by time and timeless. Understanding love requires multidimensional models. Being a loving individual requires making a choice.

Light as a Model for Love

Imagine for a moment that love was a form of energy like light. The two might be viewed in similar ways. They are highly complex, multifaceted and encourage life.

Light, like love, has dimensionality that is remarkable. It is just white light until it hits a mist or prism, which causes the colors to separate into a rainbow. White splits into red, orange, yellow, green, blue, indigo, and violet. All the colors of the spectrum appear.

Love is that way, too. It brings color to the world of the person who loves. It is also interactive and life-giving.

When plant cells interact with light, photosynthesis results, which provides the sustenance for life. Light has excited the chlorophyll to initiate life.

When people interact with love, many things can happen. As several men in the preceding chapters have shared, love for them facilitated a process of internal growth. Whether the response was immediate or delayed, many of them reported that the outcome was positive change. In some cases, it saved their lives or gave back to them a quality of life which was better than they had before.

Love and light also have a dual nature. Light is classified both as particle and wave. This means that light is sufficiently complex to behave in ways that fit two scientific classifications. In everyday life, light appears different depending on how you look at it. It is the same light, it simply gets filtered through different things. When filtered through the sky it looks blue; when into the sea it may appear green, gray or dark blue.

Love is a noun as well as a verb. It refers to an outcome (something one receives or gives) and also a process. It operates differently depending on which classification one observes. The giving (process) is often difficult to separate from the how the gift affects the giver. The two blend together.

Light and love are both forms of energy. Light is electromagnetic; love is emotional energy. Light is the source of energy that enables life; love is the source of energy that provides happiness and fulfillment.

Love and light also enhance and create natural beauty. Love sees the ordinary as exceptional, the loved one as beautiful. At sunrise and sunset, levels of light transform the ordinary into the extraordinary.

It is not the purpose of this summary to suggest that love be classified as light. It is simply that many people, including psychologists, have often missed the impact of love in people's lives. Looking at love and relationship within a person's life, they have often seen only one dimension—the light as white.

What they have missed is the multitude of colors. They have, in effect, missed the rainbow.

The men within these pages have shared some of the dimensions of their experience with vibrant colors and emotional vulnerability. The tools we have to understand and analyze them are limited. We are looking at light as white, while searching for a prism through which to view the rainbow.

Our understanding of love is still unfolding. Regardless of how well love is understood, what is important is that there are men who believe in love and choose to be loving. Within their stories there is much to be learned.

Love as Motivation

"The biggest victories in my life were motivated by love for another human being." The speaker is Howard Schukowski, a forty-five year old boiler inspector. A high school graduate and veteran, Howard reported what he views as the three major victories of his life.

Victory # 1. I stopped drinking after thirty years. I have had four years of sobriety. My love for my wife Sally motivated me to change. I didn't want to lose her. I realized I needed to try another path. Wanting that love helped me to change. Oh, initially I blamed her, but when the alcohol was out of my system, clear thinking returned. I have been in Alcoholics Anonymous and maintained my sobriety. It scares me to think how much I could have lost.

I was socialized that to be a man meant that whatever came along in life, I should be able to handle. I should be able to correct any problem and never show I was weak. Men never cry—they are tough enough to go past that. If something was wrong in life, it was assumed to be my fault and I was the one who should make it right or suffer the consequences. This was a lot to always have on my shoulders. When I reached the edge of my limits (because there will always be things one person can't handle alone), I would drink. I did this for thirty years.

Victory # 2. I stopped smoking after twenty-five years. I started smoking at age twenty, was addicted and thought I'd never be able to stop. Now, here I am, two years later, and I've maintained this change.

Victory # 3. This one I feel might be the best one of all. It's getting to know my wife Sally as a human being. I suppose it sounds silly, but this means to me that I have overcome having to be in control, even in my marriage. I now enjoy life instead of trying to control it. As a result, life is more worth living. That's a tough one—you go through life as a man thinking you have to be in charge and responsible for everything, and then you finally achieve your goal of just living life. It is amazing.

What made the difference? Through AA I learned that I don't have all the answers and it's ok to ask for help— whether it's a male or female giving you the answers. I came to realize I had more options when I realized I didn't have to do it all myself.

Through program and therapy I learned that feelings I thought were just for females were identical to those males had, too. I saw that it was ok to cry and that sometimes things happened that were not my fault. I learned a lot about alcoholism.

I also learned about fear. I realize that fear is the biggest area of my character defect. Men are socialized to never admit they're afraid. When I saw I didn't have to know it all and that fear was a normal emotion, it was a humbling experience but also enlightening.

Part of the healing for me, too, with Sally and program was the spiritual part. Love and spiritual are connected together so the more you love, the more spiritual you feel.

Oh, one other thing. Because I always felt responsible for things, I always felt I had to fix them. I had always thought it had to be an action to help somebody. Now I know listening is also a form of healing. It's a new concept for me.

Howard changed his life. He did so motivated by a desire to maintain the love he shared with his wife. Not wanting to lose her—not for practical or financial reasons but for emotional ones—was significant to him. It brought him in touch with self-awareness, and he made a choice that changed his life. Howard chose the path with love.

In looking forward to where we go from here, let us survey where we are. Men's stories have taken us through many different dimensions. We have seen the rainbow from inside.

SUMMARIZING LOVE

There are men who believe in love. They are scattered throughout different countries, social classes and educational groups. Single and married; short and tall, like the sun, they bring light and life to those around them. Whether they are born loving or whether they fight their way back from personal trauma, they believe in love because they choose to. They are the modern knights. Some are ready to stand up to challenges; some are still knights-in-training. Development and time make a difference in these men's lives. And they can change.

The ideas they have shared have been reviewed as we went along. Some of the recurrent themes are as follows.

1. There are men who believe in love and men who don't. They differ in the choices they make, the behaviors they perform, the belief systems they maintain and the mental images they retain.

2. Men who believe in love are true positives—the way they appear is the way they are. They are emotional suns bringing light and warmth. Men who don't believe in love may be false negatives (they may eventually change into men who choose love) or true negatives (they will not ever do so). Some individuals in this last group could be considered, analogous to the first image, emotional black holes who steal emotional light.

3. In order to remain loving during times of trauma, the

presence of emotional supports is important. They help to counter the damage caused by stressors. Supports can be those within the person as well as those within the situation.

4. Personal victory over trauma or obstacle may reflect a life choice. There are men to whom such victory is important. As a result, they make choices in that direction.

5. When men believe in love, they accept their emotional vulnerability and continue to pursue self-awareness. They take risks, fight to find new ways of resolving old problems and are truthful.

6. Despair scrawls on a restaurant wall: "Love's a myth, pal." Hope writes beneath it: "Only sometimes, pal." When men believe in love, they maintain hope. Belief in love is accompanied by persistence and an optimism that the sun will always come up. Love is there if you want to choose it and are willing to risk. The beauty of the rainbow is within reach.

MOVING INTO LOVE

Looking back through the chapter and the book, we see the colors of the rainbow of men's lives. Orange pain, white rage, red shame and purple courage emerge from the stories lived by these men from different parts of the globe. We see also light blues of peace and contentment; the greens of growth and personal evolving; and the yellow of joy. We see vibrant passion and shining intellect. We see the glow of goodness. The colors—separate parts of their stories—are aspects of the light of love.

At some point the colors merge for us as we make our way on. We survey the whole and see the strength of light, illuminating the shadows and sharing hope. Like the rising sun, light touches everything in its path.

Where we go from here is into the chain of people who are part of the brightness. Like these men who believe in love, having experienced emotional pain and malice, we choose not to increase human pain. We may also choose, like these men, to be a bringer of light. With that, we have one final story. It is the story of Richard. It involves the light of love.

My name is Richard Templeton and what I have to share is my story. A forty-two year old native of central England, I have lived here all my life.

I was brought up in the traditional English upper-class way, by a series of nannies. My parents were emotionally distant: I had virtually no sign of affection from my father, somewhat more from my mother, and there was very little physical contact between parents and child.

At age six I was loaded onto a train and sent to a boarding school I had never seen before. Something registered as rejection—a voice inside yelled out to them, "Don't do this." It registered hard. I was not visited by my parents, and during holidays they were often absent. I had a tremendous feeling of rejection, lack of love and sense of failure. I couldn't understand why all of these things happened, and I felt responsible for the results.

How did it change? Partly by getting away when I was eighteen; partly by meeting people from different backgrounds; most significantly from meeting my wife who really melted that away so that I was able to express what had always been there, which was a great deal of love for other people.

I experienced a paradigm shift—an extreme shift in how I viewed things. I went from darkness—being isolated and suicidal, even—to the sun coming out, and my wife was the stimulus.

What goes on before doesn't go away. In the positive, it makes one compassionate towards other people and very understanding of their problems. As a result I made an extremely clear decision that I would devote the rest of my life to communicating with other people who feel isolated so they knew they weren't alone and there was help available. I founded a publishing company and have been involved in this field ever since. I had been left some money from a trust and felt slightly guilty that I hadn't earned any of it. I wanted to convert it to a good use. It was money that somehow needed to be transformed into something I felt good about.

What effect did that have on me? Very positive. I felt I really had a place both in the world and inside of me that I could honor. Sometimes, the world was against this move, and other times it wasn't interested in what I was publishing.

Honor to me means to literally feel honorable and that has something to do with goodness. I think it has something to do with the right kind of pride in what you're doing. It is being part of something that illumines outside that matches the light you have inside. In a way, now I could do for others what my wife had done for me. I had been given an opportunity to pass on what I'd received—love from my wife—throughout the world. Sharing information through books and providing leadership in publishing is like being a bringer of light.

Chain of Light

What happens
to love
that is not returned?
Where
does it go?

There is
in the Forest of Darkness
* a touchstone*
* so bright*
* it glows.*
* Hidden there*
* in forest heart*
* it is sought*
* by pilgrims*

who travel distant lands
to reach it.

Some
never find it.

But those who do
return from the forest
with a glow
that shines
within and without
in a halo
of light. And

those they meet
along the path
they touch
with the same light
and it flows
and those
touch others
and those
touch others
until there are
hundreds of

thousands
of people
separated in
space
bound
by a chain of light.[3]

Notes

Chapter 1

1. J. M. Kouzes and B. P. Posner, *The Leadership Challenge* (San Francisco: Jossey Bass Publishers, 1988), p. 271.
2. Susan Edwards, "wonder child," in *Poems for Emotional Healing* © 1987 (unpublished manuscript).
3. Susan Edwards, "How to Tame a Woman," in *Poems for Emotional Healing* © 1987 (unpublished manuscript).
4. Henry David Thoreau, *Walden.*
5. Tom Williams, Ph.D. "The Role of Women in Showing Me the Way to Believe in Myself," 1992 (Glasgow, Scotland, unpublished paper).
6. Susan Edwards, "River of Fire," in *Poems for Emotional Healing* © 1987 (unpublished manuscript).
7. Rodney Ferris, "How Organizational Love Can Improve Leadership." *Organizational Dynamics* (Summer 1988): 40–51.
8. Jack Mendleson, *The Man Inside the Power Suit.* © 1989 (Radford, Virginia: Radford University, Department of Management).

Chapter 2

1. Susan Edwards, "How to Break a Person," in *Poems for Emotional Healing* © 1987 (unpublished manuscript).
2. Susan Edwards, "To Ed," in *Poems for Emotional Healing* © 1987 (unpublished manuscript).
3. Susan Edwards, "the stranger," in *Poems for Emotional Healing* © 1987 (unpublished manuscript).

Chapter 3

1. Information from the Encyclopedie Larousse, 1926 Edition: "Arvers (Alexis-Felix), poet and dramatic author, born and died in Paris (1806–1850). He started his literary career with a collection of poems, 'My Lost Hours' (1833), in which one finds the sonnet to which he owes the best part of his renown. It is thought that the poet had in mind Mme. Menessier, daughter of Charles Nodier."
   The citation for the sonnet is: *Larousse of the Twentieth Century* (Paris: Larousse Librairie, 1926), v. 1, p. 376. Translated in personal correspondence to the editor.
2. This song was written by the Scottish poet in 1792 for his first love Mary Campbell, who died before they could wed. She was also the inspiration for "To Mary in Heaven.'
   See George B. Woods, Homer A. Watt, George K. Anderson, *The Literature of England: An Anthology and A History.* Vol. 2 (New York: Scott Foresman, 1948), p. 108.

Chapter 4

1. Susan Edwards, "the phoenix," in *Poems for Emotional Healing* © 1987 (unpublished manuscript).
2. Clifford Swenson, *Approach to Case Conceptualization.* Guidance Monograph (Boston: Houghton Mifflin, 1968).
3. E. J. Anthony and B. J. Cohler, eds. *The Invulnerable Child* (New York: The Guilford Press, 1987).
4. J. D. Coie, N. F. Watt, S. G. West, J. D. Hawkins, J. A. Asarnow, H. J. Markham, S. L. Ramey, M. B. Shure, and B. Long, "The Science of Prevention." *American Psychologist* 48 (1993): 1013–22.
5. N. Garmezy and K. Neuchter, "Invulnerable Children—Fact and Fiction of Competence and Disadvantage." *American Journal of Orthopsychiatry*: 42 (1972): 328 N. Garmezy, "Vulnerable and Invulnerable Children: Theory, Research and Intervention." In JSAS *Catalog of Selected Documents in Psychology* 6 (1976): 96. N. Garmezy and M. Rutter, eds., *Stress, Coping and Development in Children* (New York: McGraw Hill, 1983) N. Garmezy,

"The Study of Stress and Competence in Children: A Building Block for Developmental Psychopathology", *Child Development* 55 (1984): 97–111 N. Garmezy, "Stress-Resistant Children: The Search for Protective Factors." In J.E. Stevenson, ed., *Recent Research in Developmental Psychopathology* (pp.213–33). *Journal of Child Psychology and Psychiatry* 4 (1985) Book suppl.

Chapter 5

1. Floyd Thompkins, Jr. "Enemies of the Ebony Warriors of Love." (Palo Alto: Stanford University Chapel, Stanford University, 1991).
2. Alice Walker, "While Love is Unfashionable," *Revolutionary Pebinias and Other Poems* (San Diego: Harcourt, Brace, Jovanovich Publishers, 1970), p. 68.
3. David Viscott, *Risking* (New York: Simon and Schuster, 1978).

Chapter 6

1. E. Schmitt. "Air Force Academy Zooms in on Sex Cases" *The New York Times*, New York: 5/1/94, p 1, 34.
2. Walter Fox, "What My Patients Taught Me" (unpublished manuscript).

Chapter 7

1. Susan Edwards, "For Mick" in *Poems for Emotional Healing*, © 1987 (unpublished manuscript).
2. *Webster's New World Dictionary of the American Language: College Edition* (New York: The World Publishing Company, 1962), p. 1091.
3. William Shakespeare, *The Tragedy of Romeo and Juliet* I.1.1–80.
4. Robert Frank, *Passions Within Reason: The Strategic Role of Emotions* (New York: W.W. Norton and Company, 1988).
5. Susan Edwards, "barnacle love" (unpublished poem, © 1985).

Chapter 8

1. Loren Eiseley, *The Immense Journey* (New York: Vintage Books, 1957), pp. 207–208.
2. Hans Krichels, "Snowbound" (unpublished story, © 1987).
3. Susan Edwards, "Once in awhile an eagle" in *Poems for Emotional Healing* © 1987 (unpublished manuscript).
4. Arnold A. Lazarus, *In the Mind's Eye* (New York: Guilford, 1985). A. A. Lazarus, *The Practice of Multimodal Theray* (Baltimore: Johns Hopkins University Press, 1989). A. A. Lazarus, A. Fay, and C. Lazarus, *Don't Believe It For a Moment!* (San Luis Obispo: Impact Press, 1994).
5. Jerry Vigna, *Episodes in Loving and Being Loved* (unpublished manuscript, © 1991).
6. Thomas Bullfinch, "Baucis and Philemon," in *Mythology* (New York: Dell Publishing Company, 1959), pp. 49–50.
7. Susan Edwards, "Mirror Man" in *Poems for Emotional Healing*, © 1987 (unpublished manuscript).

Chapter 9

1. Paul Andersen and Deborah Cadbury, *Imagined Worlds: Stories of Scientific Discovery* (London: Ariel Books, 1985), p. 163.
2. Robert Sternberg, "Love Is a Story" in *The General Psychologist* 30 (Spring 1994): 1–11.
3. Susan Edwards, "Chain of Light", in *Poems for Emotional Healing* © 1987 (unpublished manuscript).

Further Reading

Listed below are books which, over the years, I have found helpful
or of interest to my patients. I am sharing them in the hope you may
also find them of benefit.

Personal Growth and Change

Lazarus, Arnold, Alan Fay and Cliff Lazarus. *Don't Believe It For a
  Moment!* San Luis Obispo: Impact Press, 1994.
Lazarus, Arnold. *In the Mind's Eye.* New York: Guilford, 1985.
Rubin, Theodore I. *Emotional Common Sense.* New York:
  Harper/Collins, 1986.
Viscott, David. *The Language of Feelings.* New York: Morrow,
  1983.

Men / Personal Growth

Bly, Robert. *Iron John.* New York: Addison-Wesley, 1990; Element,
  UK, 1990.
Drew, Jane M. *Where Were You When I Needed You Dad? A Guide
  for Healing Your Father Wound.* Minnetonka, Minnesota: Tiger
  Lily Press, 1992.
Keen, Sam. *The Passionate Life: Stages of Loving.* San Francisco:
  Harper, 1983.
Shain, Merle. *Some Men Are More Perfect Than Others.* New York:
  Bantam: 1980.

Relationship Psychology

Fay, Allen. *PQR: Prescription for a Quality Relationship*. New York: Multimodal Press, 1988.
Viscott, David. *How to Live With Another Person*. New York: Pocket Books, 1983.

General Reference

National Men's Resource Center. National resource center on men's issues, information and referral. P.O. Box 800-SH, San Anselmo, CA 94979-0800. Call (415) 453-2839.

Index